Consent and Consensus

Key Concepts in Political Science

GENERAL EDITOR: Leonard Schapiro
EXECUTIVE EDITOR: Peter Calvert

Other titles in the same series include:

ALREADY PUBLISHED

Martin Albrow	**Bureaucracy**
Peter Calvert	**Revolution**
Brian Chapman	**Police State**
Ioan Davies	**Social Mobility and Political Change**
Joseph Frankel	**National Interest**
P. H. Partridge	**Consent and Consensus**
John Plamenatz	**Ideology**

IN PREPARATION

Shlomo Avineri	**Utopianism**
Stanley Benn	**Power**
Anthony H. Birch	**Representation**
Karl Deutsch	**Legitimacy**
S. E. Finer	**Dictatorship**
C. J. Friedrich	**Tradition and Authority**
Geoffrey Goodwin	**International Society**
Julius Gould	**Violence**
E. Kamenka and Alice Erh-Soon Tay	**Law**
J. F. Lively	**Democracy**
Robert Orr	**Liberty**
John C. Rees	**Equality**
Leonard Schapiro	**Totalitarianism**
Henry Tudor	**Political Myth**

Consent and Consensus

P. H. Partridge

Praeger Publishers
New York · Washington · London

Published in the United States of America in 1971

Praeger Publishers, Inc.
111 Fourth Avenue, New York, N.Y. 10003, U.S.A.
5 Cromwell Place, London, S.W.7, England

© 1971 by Pall Mall Press Limited, London, England
Library of Congress Catalog Card Number: 75-95685

Printed in Great Britain

Contents

'Key Concepts'
an Introductory Note   7

1/The Problem of Consent   9

2/The Meaning of Consent   28

3/The Anatomy of Consent   49

4/Theories of Consensus   71

5/Consensus and Democracy   96

6/Consensus, Dissent and Ideology   120

7/A Last Word about Consent   139

Notes and References   153

Bibliography   157

Index   161

'Key Concepts'
an Introductory Note

Political concepts are part of our daily speech—we abuse 'bureaucracy' and praise 'democracy', welcome or recoil from 'revolution'. Emotive words such as 'equality', 'dictatorship', 'élite' or even 'power' can often, by the very passions which they raise, obscure a proper understanding of the sense in which they are, or should be, or should not be, or have been used. Confucius regarded the 'rectification of names' as the first task of government. 'If names are not correct, language will not be in accordance with the truth of things', and this in time would lead to the end of justice, to anarchy and to war. One could with some truth point out that the attempts hitherto by governments to enforce their own quaint meanings on words have not been conspicuous for their success in the advancement of justice. 'Rectification of names' there must certainly be: but most of us would prefer such rectification to take place in the free debate of the university, in the competitive arena of the pages of the book or journal.

Analysis of commonly used political terms, their reassessment or their 'rectification', is, of course, normal activity in the political science departments of our universities. The idea of this series was indeed born in the course of discussion between a few university teachers of political science, of whom Professor S. E. Finer of Manchester University was one. It occurred to us that a series of short books discussing the 'Key Concepts' in political science would serve two purposes. In universities these books could provide the kind of brief political texts which might be of assistance to students in gaining a fuller understanding of the terms which they were constantly using. But we also hoped that outside the universities there exists a reading public which has the time, the curiosity and the inclination to pause to reflect on some of those words and ideas which are so often taken for granted. Perhaps even 'that insidious and crafty animal', as Adam Smith described the politican and statesman, will occasionally derive some pleasure or even profit from that more leisurely analysis which academic study can afford, and which a busy life in the practice of politics often denies.

It has been very far from the minds of those who have been concerned in planning and bringing into being the 'Key Concepts' series to try and impose (as if that were possible!) any uniform pattern on the authors who have contributed, or will contribute, to it. I, for one, hope that each author will, in his own individual manner, seek and find the best way of helping us to a fuller understanding of the concept which he has chosen to analyse. But whatever form the individual exposition may take, there are, I believe, three aspects of illumination which we can confidently expect from each volume in this series. First, we can look for some examination of the history of the concept, and of its evolution against a changing social and political background. I believe, as many do who are concerned with the study of political science, that it is primarily in history that the explanation must be sought for many of the perplexing problems of political analysis and judgement which beset us today. Second, there is the semantic aspect. To look in depth at a 'key concept' necessarily entails a study of the name which attached itself to it; of the different ways in which, and the different purposes for which, the name was used; of the way in which in the course of history the same name was applied to several concepts, or several names were applied to one and the same concept; and, indeed, of the changes which the same concept, or what appears to be the same concept, has undergone in the course of time. This analysis will usually require a searching examination of the relevant literature in order to assess the present stage of scholarship in each particular field. And thirdly, I hope that the reader of each volume in this series will be able to decide for himself what the proper and valid use should be of a familiar term in politics, and will gain, as it were, from each volume a sharper and better-tempered tool of political analysis.

There are many today who would disagree with Bismarck's view that politics can never be an exact science. I express no opinion on this much debated question. But all of us who are students of politics—and our numbers both inside and outside the universities continue to grow—will be the better for knowing what precisely we mean when we use a common political term.

London School of Economics   Leonard Schapiro
and Political Science   General Editor

1/The Problem of Consent

The doctrine that governments ought to be founded on the consent of the governed, that only those governments which enjoy the consent of their subjects possess rightful authority and can legitimately demand or expect obedience, is one that we naturally think of as an essential part of a democratic position. Indeed, in the most recent period of the history of political thought 'government with the consent of the governed' has commonly been one of the slogans or formulas that specify the nature of a democratic system and distinguish it from those that are non-democratic. Men are politically free only when they consent to the authority of their governments.

Whether, however, such a formulation is a sufficient characterization of the distinctive quality of a democratic system is very dubious, and, even if we take 'government by the consent of the governed' to be a necessary but not a sufficient specification of what democracy requires, the concept of consent needs very considerable amplification and interpretation before we can see at all clearly how the doctrine is to be applied or what claims it does precisely make. 'Consent', like many general terms of political theory and apologetics, is capable of a multitude of ambiguities and meanings, but unlike some of those other terms—freedom or equality or justice, for example—it has not been subject to anything like the same intense philosophical scrutiny. It is surprising that, considering its wide currency, especially in the ideology and rhetoric of democracy, it has not been more frequently the subject of those close and sustained conceptual examinations in which modern philosophers delight.

Yet, although the natural tendency today is to link the concept of consent with modern democratic positions, with doctrines of political freedom and popular government, and thereby to import into it some of the content people derive from their familiarity with parliamentary elections, political parties and representative government, it would be an error to assume that its birth coincided more or less with the birth of movements of thought recognizably democratic to us. On the contrary, some sort of notion of consent as describing the relation of subjects with their government and of members of a political society with one another has been present throughout virtually the whole history of political speculation. If we consider its persistence or ubiquity we are tempted to say that it is one of the most basic and inescapable of the ideas in terms of which men think about the nature of government and the qualities of a political society.

Throughout the history of social thought, consent and consensus have been ideas both persistent and elusive: persistent, because there have been thinkers in all times who have held that there must be an element of agreement or consensus in the constitution of human society; and elusive, because these thinkers have always found it difficult to specify what the nature of that consensus may be. In our own day there has been less discussion of the idea of consent but for modern sociologists, including political sociologists, consensus has become more than ever a debated and debatable idea.

The idea that human society somehow depends on a voluntary agreement by its members to associate for the achievement of common goods, and upon the voluntary acceptance of mutual rights and common arrangements, is one of great antiquity. Of equal antiquity is the notion that political authority is created by, and is sustained by, the will and consent of the governed. We are most familiar, perhaps, with these two ideas in the doctrine of the social contract, the origins of which are Greek, and which played an important role in Western political thinking at least to the eighteenth century.

Historians of this doctrine have usually distinguished two different forms of the contract in the thought of the social contract theorists: the social contract itself, by which individuals agree to form themselves into an organized society; and the contract of government, by which the members of a society institute and place themselves under the rule of a political authority for the purpose of better achieving their common good.[1] Both of these forms of the contract introduce the idea that society itself, and also government, rest on the consent of the members of a society, and upon some measure of agreement or consensus among them. Thus, the history of the ideas of consent and consensus can be traced, in part, within the history of the social contract doctrine; but only in part because, as we shall shortly see, the idea that political authority derives its legitimacy from the consent of those over whom it is exercised could also be propounded by writers who did not think of government as being a matter of a contract or compact between the rulers and the ruled.

Some historians of the contract link its origins with a distinction, very important within Greek philosophical and social thought, between 'nature' and 'convention'. This contrasts what may be said to exist 'by nature' and that which is 'conventional' or the result of human contrivance. Some of the Sophists with whom Socrates contends in *The Republic* and other dialogues held that man is not social 'by nature' but that society is 'conventional' or a matter of human decision and contrivance. They held also that the laws which men obey are not established by 'nature' or part of the 'natural' order of things, but are rules contrived by men themselves for their various purposes. This distinction between 'natural' and 'conventional' is present in that distinction between 'the state of nature' and 'civil society' upon which the social contract theorists of the seventeenth and eighteenth centuries based themselves. For many centuries it was *one* of the philosophical supports invoked by those who argued that both society and government were the products of human beings deliberately seeking ways to achieve their own good; and that government, having been constituted by men for their own purposes, necessarily owed its power and authority to their agreement or consent.

Neither Plato nor Aristotle, the two greatest social thinkers of classical times, accepted the notion of the 'conventional' origin or character of organized society and its laws. Aristotle's assertion that man is by nature a political animal is one of the most famous political propositions in the history of social thought. Aristotle meant that it is only by membership of a politically organized community that man can realize his true end or 'nature'; outside of such a society he is not properly speaking a man at all. In his *Politics* Aristotle provides what might be described as a 'naturalistic' account of the development of the political community, tracing the manner in which smaller social communities such as the family and the smaller groups reach their fulfilment within the complete, self-subsistent, political community. Thus, Aristotle does not derive society nor the authority of the political community from any pre-social agreement or decision by the members. Yet he believed that the life and strength of the *polis* required a strong community of purpose among those who belonged to it. As C. H. McIlwain expounds Aristotle's conception of the *polis*: 'There must be a common object of all their lives if citizens are ever truly to "live together" as members of a *koinonia* instead of merely feeding together like the cattle in one field. That object, Aristotle says, is "the safety of the *polity*", and by this he means nothing less than a common devotion to the central principle of the community's life . . .'[2] In modern terminology, Aristotle held that the existence of the *polis* in its most developed form required a high measure of consensus: a devotion on the part of its members to the *polis* itself, its good, its institutions, the values embodied in its institutions.

One difference between classical political thought and that of the last four centuries is that one finds in the former little trace of the individualism, and the connected emphasis on the rights that individuals possess as such and which may need to be asserted and protected against the community and the political authority. These *have* been important themes in Western thought since the seventeenth century. In modern political thought, the idea of government by the consent of the governed is frequently linked, of course, with the notion of individual rights to be protected. Greek political thinkers, including Plato and Aristotle, and the philosophers of the early Middle Ages, were not preoccupied by these more developed individualist conceptions. They tended to think more of the community as a unified and cohesive whole; and they were interested in discerning the nature of the political community, its importance for the moral life of its members, and the principles of cohesion by which it was unified. The idea of a community bonded together by something that might be called the consent of its members was not absent either from classical thought or from that of the early medieval period; but the notion of consent in the sense of 'individual acceptance by each and every human being acting as a unit'[3] clearly emerged only much later, perhaps not earlier than the fifteenth century.

Thus, there is a famous sentence in Cicero's *De Republica* in which he defines the nature of political society: 'Quid est enim civitas nisi juris societias?', which McIlwain translates as 'partnership in law', the state being defined as 'an assemblage of men associated in consent to law'. According to Gough, 'Cicero seems to have held that while the state involves a common will and consent, it is an organic development from the natural association of the family, and can rightly command the loyalty of its members.'[4] Thus, in such views as these 'consent' is not identified with a deliberate decision to constitute a society, even though it may be a necessary element in the corporate unity of a community. Similarly, in the early Middle Ages the community seems to have been conceived of as the coherent or cohesive unit of social life; and custom or law (law being usually thought of as customary in its nature) thought of as expressing the life of the community and its will. Early medieval ideas of kingship usually depicted the king as bound to maintain the laws and customs of his people, and as requiring the consent of his people (or of men of power and wisdom supposed to speak for them) for changes in law or custom. Gough speaks of the pervasive principle of government among the Teutonic kingdoms of early medieval Europe that 'the king was no absolute or arbitrary ruler, but that the allegiance owed to him by his subjects was dependent on his recognising their rights, and that in his legislative capacity he could only make laws after getting the advice and consent of his wise men, and in some sense of his whole people'.[5]

During the first ten centuries of the Christian era the assumption that kingship is elective, that the king is enthroned and rules with the consent of the people, was widely accepted. Historians of political thought cite coronation oaths and much other material to show how strongly the idea of elective monarchy was implanted. There is usually present an embryonic conception of a contract or compact: the people promise loyalty and obedience to the king, he promises to maintain the laws and rights of his subjects. The doctrine of popular election could, it seems, be comfortably combined with the institution of hereditary succession and with the belief that royal power is divinely constituted: according to A. J. Carlye, in the ninth century 'the divine appointment, the custom of hereditary succession, the election by the great men and the people—all these elements go to constitute the conception of a legitimate claim to the throne'.[6]

Thus, the theory that political authority derived from the consent of subjects or citizens was perhaps more familiar in the Middle Ages than it came to be in the seventeenth and eighteenth centuries. In the earlier period, it was supported by other political traditions. One was the Roman law tradition; according to Carlyle, 'the great jurists of the Digest recognised one, and only one, source of political authority in the Empire, that is, the Roman people, and the emperors themselves, as late as Justinian, acknowledged this as the true theory'. At a later time, stimulated by the conflict between the Empire and the Papacy, and also by movements for the reform of government within the Church, the idea of the popular sanction of supreme authority came to be stated still more sharply, and to be applied to the government of the Church itself. Thus, Marsiglio of Padua, who was opposing ecclesiastical pretensions to secular authority, and whose *Defensor Pacis* was published in the early fourteenth century, argued that 'the legislator, or the proper and efficient cause of law, is the whole body of citizens or the prevailing part of it, commanding or deciding by its own choice or will in a general assembly and in set terms that something among the civil acts of human beings be done or omitted, on pain of penalty or temporal punishment'.[7] Similarly, early in the fifteenth century, Nicholas of Cusa, supporting the reform of church government, asserted that 'since by nature all men are free, any authority by which subjects are prevented from doing evil and their freedom is restrained . . . comes solely from harmony and from the consent of the subjects . . . For if by nature men are equally strong and equally free, the true and settled power of one over the others, the ruler having equal natural power, could be set up only by the choice and consent of the others, just as law also is set up by consent.'[8]

These few references may suffice to illustrate the ubiquity throughout the Middle Ages of the idea that supreme political authority, even though it may be, in some sense, 'of God', was made legitimate by the free consent or acceptance of 'the people'. No doubt, these medieval ideas of consent were usually shadowy and unspecified: they were linked with rudimentary conceptions of constitutional government (with the demand that kings should uphold or rule in accordance with the law); but, of course, seldom or not at all with concrete notions about the actual exercise of popular power. And it would not be easy to spell out in, for example, the context of medieval ideas about elective monarchy, just what the 'consent' of the community might mean.

In the sixteenth and seventeenth centuries the concept of consent began to get a sharper edge. With the appearance of the embryonic national states of western Europe, the emergence of the absolute monarchs, and the development of the doctrine of 'divine right' to justify unlimited monarchical authority, theories of consent, in various forms, were asserted to counter the pretensions of absolute kings and as a means of claiming inalienable individual rights and liberties. In the seventeenth century the doctrine of popular consent joined forces with the doctrine of natural rights. And even as early as the seventeenth century we find evidence (for example in England among the radical movements of the Civil War years), of the linking of the ancient notion of political authority as deriving from the consent of the people with the demand for wider popular sharing in the exercise of political power. We may say that, from then on, the idea of government with the consent of the governed becomes absorbed into the ideology of modern democracy.

We mentioned earlier two forms of the social contract theory: the agreement by which individuals form and maintain themselves in an organized society, and the contract of government. These two forms correspond to two different contexts within which the idea of consent can be employed. The few examples of medieval political thinking mentioned were concerned with consent as the basis of legitimate political authority. In societies as profoundly steeped in tradition and custom as those of the Middle Ages, we would not expect the idea that society is itself the product of deliberate decision and agreement to be as prominent as the other notion that political rule is sustained by the free acceptance of the community. Nevertheless, the doctrine that society is itself a voluntary association was not unheard of in Greek and Roman times; and we may say that the two traditions of social thought ran together and were intermingled. We may select Richard Hooker's *The Laws of Ecclesiastical Polity*, the greater part of which was published right at the end of the sixteenth century, as an especially interesting example of the intermingling of these two traditions of thought.

Hooker holds both that there is a 'natural' foundation for human society and also that society can be established only by agreement or consent. 'Two foundations there are which bear up public societies; the one, a natural inclination, whereby all men desire a sociable life and fellowship; and the other, an order expressly or secretly agreed upon touching the manner of their living together.'[9] There is no impossibility 'in nature considered by itself but that men might have lived without any public regiment',[10] it is the 'corruption of our nature' that makes that unachievable; and so 'the law of nature doth now require of necessity some kind of regiment'.[11] 'Men always knew that strifes and troubles would be endless except they gave their common consent all to be ordered by some whom they should agree upon . . . So that in a word all public regiment of what kind soever seemeth evidently to have arisen from deliberate advice, consultation, and composition between men, judging it convenient and behoveful.'[12]

Hooker also speaks of '. . . whatsoever hath been after in free and voluntary manner condescended unto, whether by express consent, whereof positive laws are witnesses, or else by silent allowance famously notified through custom reaching beyond the memory of man'.[13] What is interesting in such a passage is a concept of consent much wider than that embodied in the works of those who are more explicitly and specifically exponents of the idea of the social contract. It is a consent that does not necessarily express itself in the particular act of agreement by which a government is set up, but which is manifested in 'custom reaching beyond the memory of man'. It expresses itself in customs which relate presumably not only to those that prescribe the exercise of political authority but also to those which regulate all the important relationships and transactions of the members of the society. And the treatment of custom or usage as manifesting consent—'silent allowance'— appears to have been a familiar mode of thinking in medieval times. When medieval kings in their coronation oaths swore to maintain the laws and customs of a people, the laws and customs were prac- tices in which the freedom of a people were expressed—something that belonged to the people and embodied their 'silently allowed' agreements concerning their manner of living together.

There are several points illustrated by the sort of position that Hooker represents that are worth noting. An agreement so specific that it may be analogous to a contract is only one way in which 'consent' may be expressed. For Hooker, as for many of his pre- decessors, the idea of the social contract is often vaguely pointed to within a wider, more general and much more indeterminate notion of the 'consent' which is the foundation of all human society. Second, Hooker is not concerned to make a sharp distinction be- tween the formation (or constitution) of society as such and the establishment of government. The two things are parts of the same process; the order men agree upon touching the manner of their living together puts them simultaneously into society and under government. Third, Hooker experiences no intellectual discomfort in gliding immediately from 'express consent' which produces 'positive laws' to 'silent allowance' which is manifested in im- memorial custom: positive law and custom are treated together as being founded on free and voluntary agreement. And fourth, 'silent allowance' itself is taken without any difficulty as falling within the category of what has been 'in free and voluntary manner condescended to'.

Clearly this leaves 'consent' hard to define. According to Hooker, the human desire for social living is not sufficient to bring society into existence or sustain it; what is also necessary is the will to live in society, the decision to make it, and a series of agreements that order and support it. It is impossible for us to conceive of custom as being the product of will and deliberate decision; and when Hooker includes custom within his account of the 'order expressly or secretly agreed upon' we may say that he is perhaps employing a concept not unlike that notion of 'consensus' which is used by some modern sociologists to explain the cohesiveness of a society—a form of agreement that falls short of explicitly expressed consent but which nevertheless represents a willing acceptance of what is the subject of the consensus. And when Roman lawyers combine the absolute authority of the emperor with the idea that his power derives from the consent of the people; or when theorists of medieval kingship assume or assert that the authority of the king is in some manner dependent upon or ratified by the acceptance of the people, it is scarcely express choice or deliberate authorization to which they are referring, but rather this much less determinate consensus: a sense that the authority of the ruler somehow flows at least in part from the fact that his subjects allow or acknowledge it. Viewed as the foundation of a theory of political obligation, it is hard to say what exact claim to political or civil rights on behalf of the subjects is implied in this conception. It seems to amount to no more than a general assumption that, because allowance or acknowledgement by subjects is a basis of the authority of the ruler, the subjects can legitimately expect that their interests and established rights will be observed by the emperor or king and that they have ground for protest or even resistance when this understanding between ruler and subjects is breached.

As has been said, the doctrine of contract was but one form in which the idea of consent manifested itself in political thought from earliest times down to a very recent period. The contract theorists, especially those of the seventeenth and eighteenth centuries such as Althusius, Grotius, Pufendorf and Locke, attempted to spell out in more specific terms the nature or meaning of the consent which was binding upon rulers. This greater specification has several aspects. On the one hand, by the time of the contractarians of the seventeenth and eighteenth centuries, vaguer and more inchoate notions about consent have joined the full stream of natural right doctrine and therefore contract theorists are concerned to define a little more explicitly the sense in which government is based upon the consent of the governed, the rights of individuals which governments are established to protect and the consequential limits of the authority which is conferred on rulers or to which subjects may be presumed to consent. On the other hand, the great seventeenth- and eighteenth-century contract theorists are more uncompromisingly individualistic, more secular, and generally freer or more disposed to conceive of government as being instituted solely for the benefit of the governed. Consequently they more often took the position that the sole source and justification of the authority of governement are to be found in the consent of the governed.

Whereas in Hooker and other earlier writers we can discern an effort to read into the customs, institutions and practices of societies dominated by religious or traditional beliefs and sentiments a consensual interpretation, the seventeenth- and eighteenth-century contract theorists are men of a more 'rationalistic' temper. They tend to present the idea that government is an essentially human contrivance in a blunter, less equivocal form; and they tend accordingly to advance the idea of consent as being at once the force to which governments owe their existence and also the source or condition of their rightful authority in a manner which is both uncompromising and highly simplified. And this is true not only of an orthodox contractarian such as John Locke, but also of radical Puritans and other forerunners of radical democracy in the seventeenth and eighteenth centuries. The Putney debates yield some of the most forthright early assertions of the doctrine that man has a duty of obedience only to those governments which he has consented to or set up over himself. There is, for example, the famous declaration of George Rainborough that '. . . the poorest he that is in England hath a life to live as the greatest he; and therefore truly, Sir, I think that every man that is to live under a government ought first by his own consent to put himself under that government'. Or there is John Wildman's, 'I conceive that's the undeniable maxim of government: that all government is in the free consent of the people. If so . . . there is no person that is under a just government unless he by his own free consent be put under that government.'

Of the leading contract theorists, Locke is usually taken to be especially the exponent of the theory that the authority of government is derived from and depends upon the consent of the governed. Hobbes's relation to the notion of consent is, of course, much more equivocal. It is true that, since he finds the origin of government in the decision and agreement of those who institute it, he may be said to hold that government comes into existence and continues to operate with the consent of the governed; but the powers that are accorded to the sovereign by the original contract are so extensive that the consent accorded to them by his subjects thereafter is consent only in one of its more Pickwickian senses. Locke owes his standing in the history of the doctrine of consent partly to the fact that his influence, exercised throughout the eighteenth century, contributed to the emergence of the later more democratic strains of thought in which the 'consent of the governed' became a central slogan. He is more important, however, because of his stronger insistence on inalienable individual rights—life, liberty and property—and because, therefore, 'consent of the governed' seemed to be associated with an impenetrable core of individual right and freedom, with 'liberty against government', and with the tight curbing of governmental power.

It is worth adding a little more about the doctrine of the social contract in order to discern the idea of consent embedded in it. As has been said, in the writing of seventeenth- and eighteenth-century contract theorists the idea of consent tends to assume a more central place in the theory of government, and it tends to be formulated in a more specific form. In Hobbes, Locke and others there is first an extreme individualism which asserts that since 'by nature' all men are free and equal, no man can have a right to exercise rule or authority over another except with the latter's consent. As Locke says, 'Reason is plain on our side that men are naturally free.' And since every man is 'naturally free . . . nothing [is] able to put him in subjection to an earthly power, but only his own consent'. It has been argued that such a doctrine leads potentially to anarchist conclusions, or makes the notion of government a contradiction in terms. It is said that, according to Locke, if any man accepts political authority it must be by his own consent; if he subordinates himself to government this must be a voluntary act; and, if this is so, then there is in effect no authority, because authority which can claim obedience only when I choose to obey it is a contradiction in terms. But to argue in this way is to give to 'consent' an interpretation which other writers may have given it but which ignores the force of the idea of 'contract' altogether. Locke says in effect that men in the state of nature have entered into an agreement to allow others to exercise authority over them or rule them within limits defined by the terms of the compact. The contract, in short, is a permission for others to exercise certain powers; in making it, natural men have transferred to others their own right to make decisions on prescribed matters and within prescribed limits. It is a general permission or consent to others to exercise authority, and, so long as those to whom power has been transferred use their power within the terms of the contract, those who have given it are under an obligation to obey.

There *are* organizations or associations in which members authorize a few of their number to govern on their behalf; the idea of consent embodied in the historical fiction of the social contract is a perfectly intelligible one. The trouble is, of course, that it can scarcely be supposed to apply to a political association—the state. The succeeding generations of men within a state do not by any explicit granting of permission renew the institutions of government from time to time; they do not from time to time define within the terms of a compact the objects and limits of the authority conferred upon their political authorities; and within any actually existing state it is always safe to assume that there is a minority of dissidents who would contest, if they could, the right of these particular rulers or this particular regime to exercise power. Hume knew these objections and his argument that popular acquiescence to governmental power leads in the course of time to the habit of obedience is a step toward a more realistic sociology of government.

Locke himself saw the more obvious difficulties. Patently, not every man does or could or would express his willing consent to the compact which establishes and defines the conditions of government and explicitly avows his willingness to be a member of the political society and to obey the established authorities. To require this as a condition of the legitimate exercise of authority and of the existence of a duty to obey would indeed be to reduce the concept of authority to a shadow. Locke, of course, is aware of this and to meet these difficulties he brings in two supplementary ideas: first, that natural men in agreeing to form themselves into a political society may be presumed at the same time to have agreed to place themselves under the authority of the majority; and second the idea of 'tacit consent'.

Locke asks 'how far anyone shall be looked on to have consented, and thereby submitted to any government, where he has made no expression of it at all'. He replies 'that every man that hath any possession or enjoyment of any part of the dominions of any government doth thereby give his tacit consent, and is so far forth obliged to obedience to the laws of that government, during such enjoyment, as anyone under it, whether this his possession be of land to him and his heirs for ever, or a lodging only for a week; or whether it is barely travelling freely on the highway; and, in effect, it reaches as far as the very being of anyone within the territories of that government'.[14] This is a clear enough position: if a man chooses to own property within a particular state which is subject to the laws of that state, or even if he chooses to remain within its territories, we may impute to him a voluntary submission to its laws, since, if he has not made an express agreement to be a member of the state, he is free to go elsewhere. Locke has already argued that 'a child is born a subject of no country or government'; therefore, his becoming a member of one rather than another is the result of an act always expressive of free choice or consent.

Locke's account of 'tacit consent' has not impressed his commentators although, as we shall see, more sophisticated and elaborate contemporary expositions of the meaning of government by consent make use of notions of tacit consent perhaps no less facile than his. And 'tacit consent' in Locke, like Hooker's 'secret allowances' and the vaguer adumbrations of consent in medieval doctrines of kingship, point forward to ideas of consensus to be found in the work of much more recent political sociologists—and leave the same questions unanswered. Obviously, what is unsatisfactory in Locke's exposition of tacit consent is the implied premise that, since any man is free to transfer himself to any other territory, his residence in one may be taken to express his own choice, an implied consent to the regime and laws he is living under. If we take this as being in part a specification of the meaning of 'consent' within the more complex idea of government based on the consent of the governed, the most obvious and serious objection is that for the large majority of men the costs of transferring to another country are so high (even if the legal freedom of exit and entry Locke assumes does exist) that the freedom Locke relies upon is a fiction. Or, putting the argument in other terms, since the costs or disincentives connected with the alternative of migration are so steep, we would be unwilling to say of the majority of those who choose to remain in their native country that they have necessarily chosen freely, that their continued residence necessarily amounts to consent. 'Tacit consent' could include a wide spectrum of different cases or individual attitudes and situations, ranging from a very free, very deliberate act of choice, through the following of custom or habit, passivity or indifference, down to a resentful or rebellious acquiescence in a hateful regime. So wide a notion of consent leaves the theory of government by consent of the governed without any particular point; one who claims that government should be authorized by the consent of the governed will need a more precise idea of consent than this.

We should not take 'tacit consent' in Locke too seriously. What is essential in his theory of government or political obligation is the claim that government is, or ought to be, established or maintained by the free choice and consent of the governed, to serve their purposes (according to Locke, 'the securing and regulating of property'). 'Tacit consent' is no more really than a saving hypothesis, brought in to meet the difficulty that *in fact* men do not expressly declare their consent to the regime under which they live— popular acceptance of a government and its laws is scarcely to be regarded as what Renan declared a nation to be, a 'plebiscite de tous les jours'. It would be unrealistic to imagine that the authority of a government, and still more the general constitution of the political authority of a state, could be explicitly and regularly renewed by expressions of consent by the governed. (It remains to be considered whether periodical elections can properly be regarded as amounting to this.) On the other hand 'tacit consent', at least in Locke, describes attitudes and situations which would hardly qualify as 'consent' for those who maintain that government should be carried on always with the consent of the governed. Thus, Locke's account of consent does not provide a set of principles or criteria which are useful when we try to fit the idea of government by the consent of the governed to modern nations and states. What remains of his teaching (so far as the doctrine of government by consent is concerned) is the broad intimation that only those governments are really legitimate which enjoy the voluntary obedience of their subjects.

But these brief comments on Locke may suggest some of the

main requirements of a useful theory of consent. Historically, the idea emerged as a theory of political obligation. As we shall see, the idea of 'government by the consent of the governed' is so complex and tricky when we try to spell it out in detail that there are many difficulties in putting it forward as an absolute ground of the duty of political obedience. In any case, the traditional problem of political obligation does not now preoccupy political philosophers nearly as much as it once did; the question why, or under what conditions, are we obliged to obey the state is not now usually regarded by political philosophers as a profitable way of approaching an examination of the nature of the state. But the idea of 'consent' has survived rather as a constituent element of democratic ideology: as a specification of an essential characteristic of democratic regimes which distinguish them from the non-democratic. Obviously, if 'consent' is to be a useful idea in this context, it must be possible to demonstrate that there prevails in democratic regimes a relationship between the governed and their government which is not present in non-democratic regimes—a relationship which without distortion of language can be described as one of consenting.

Thus, one problem is to show that there is a sense in which democratic states *are* characterized by the consent of the governed, and that this is consent in some significant sense. It would not do, for example, if 'consent' is no more than the acquiescence or habitual, complacent obedience that may characterize the subjects of a tyranny, or the passionate but unquestioning identification with a ruler or dominant ideology that may be present in highly authoritarian states. If these are admissible forms of consent, then consent is useless as a specification of the special character of a democratic system. This is the objection to Locke's 'tacit consent': it does not necessarily exclude tyranny or authoritarianism. A similar point may be made in connection with the notions of consensus and legitimacy employed by some sociologists in theories of the bases of political authority. One can speak quite properly about 'legitimate authority' in the sociologists' sense as authority which is acknowledged as such by the members of the social group over whom it is exercised. One may also say that the 'legitimacy' of an authority derives from the social consensus in which the rightful authority of the ruler is generally recognized. But this cannot necessarily be the 'consent' of which democratic ideologists or theorists have spoken because these sentiments of legitimacy may be felt in regimes commonly classified as non-democratic. And, as a matter of fact, some at least of the totalitarian or highly authoritarian regimes of this century seem to have been supported, at least for a time, by powerful sentiments of legitimacy widely shared among the citizens.

Consent, therefore, must be intended to mean something other than willing or unforced acquiescence. On the other hand, if there is to be any point in the notion of government by the consent of the governed as defining one type of political regime, we will expect it to be more than a utopian idea, i.e. one that could not be exemplified in a complex modern state. Obviously there are many associations small enough to manage their affairs with the participation and consent of their members. Communities compact enough to be governed by the 'town meeting' may achieve the ideal of government with the consent of the governed. Rousseau held that any community ruled by the authority of the 'general will' (and his was in a sense a doctrine of government by consent, but of a special kind that departed far from ordinary notions of consent) must be small enough to enable all its members to take part in the making of decisions and he would not allow that representative government could be government by the 'general will'. But such conceptions are of small relevance here. The states with which we must concern ourselves are characterized by their great geographical extent, the size of their populations and other qualities which are at first sight just as unpromising to the idea of government by consent. Their complexity includes the enormous variety of organizations, groups, activities, aspirations and interests that divide their populations. And there is the speed with which conditions within these states develop and change, the rapidity with which problems needing the attention of governments emerge and the need for incessant activity and continuous decision to cope with them. Is it conceivable that societies so constituted can transact the business of politics and government so as to secure always the consent of the governed in any significant degree?

One characteristic of the states which have emerged since Locke wrote makes a delineation of the meaning of consent more difficult. Nothing like the full force of the idea of democracy was, of course apparent to him. From the standpoint of his extreme individualism the functions of government were minimal. Men entered society from the state of nature, equipped with their bundle of natural rights, and the central function of government was to provide protection or security. It was only later that the idea of a government incessantly occupied with legislative activity, one that existed to give effective expression to the constantly evolving demands and 'needs' of the body of citizens, emerged fully in conception and in historical fact. It is one thing to say that a government should be founded on the consent of the governed when its chief duty is to administer and protect a social order already more or less established and agreed upon. But it is a different thing to make that claim in regard to a government that is charged with the obligation to be constantly innovating, making and executing policy designed to advance the 'welfare' of its subjects. It is obvious that a government that is always disturbing and modifying existing arrangements of activities, relationships and rights must find more trouble in retaining the consent of the governed than the relatively 'inactive' or conservative governments that individualistic, natural-right theorists such as Locke had in mind.

There are some contemporary political philosophers who have concluded that the doctrine of 'consent of the governed' is no more than an impractical ideal. Or perhaps that it is an ideological slogan which, like many of the central terms of any political ideology, has a limited plausibility when employed to describe and justify the characteristics of a political order, but which mainly distracts attention away from or conceals the true nature of that order. It would not be hard to make out a fairly convincing case for that conclusion. It is true, as we have remarked, that there have been surprisingly few attempts by political philosophers to spell out in any detail the meaning of consent as it is supposed to be realized within the arrangements and processes of democratic systems. Most democratic ideologists have allowed 'consent' to remain a vague, unanalysed generality, only very loosely and equivocally connected with the practice of democratic systems and even apparently contradicted by many of their accepted arrangements. There is some justification for those writers who have concluded that 'consent' is not an accurate or useful specification of a democratic regime, and that the important qualities of democracy would be better defined in a different manner.

But this is not the conclusion we shall argue for in this book. We shall argue that the concept of the 'consent of the governed' does indicate something important in the working of a political system; that may be present or absent; that represents a significant difference between some states and others. Yet it is not an easy matter to adapt the idea of consent to all the complexities of a modern state. In such states it is not likely that 'consent' will be a simple direct relation between the members of society and their government, the kind of direct relation one might find between the members and those who exercise authority in an association of a couple of dozen members. (Sometimes difficulties in making sense of the concept of consent have been connected with assumptions of such a simplified model.) When we take account of the nature, range and variety of governmental activity in a contemporary state we can see at once that 'consent', if any such thing does exist at all, must be a very complex affair. And similarly when we take account of the complexity of social structure and organization also. The members of a modern society perform activities and live lives within many different associations and organizations which often exercise control over them, administer them and not infrequently represent them in negotiations with government and in more general participation in the processes of political life. Thus, a man's judgement concerning the degree of freedom and responsibility he enjoys, the extent to which he has to endure interference, restraint or oppression, whether or not the authorities which shape his life are legitimate authorities, may well be as much a judgement of his situation within one or another of these 'special' organizations or associations as of his situation as a subject member of the state. It is a commonplace that the political processes of modern states flow through an extremely pluralistic complex of associations, institutions and organizations; and also that it is a function of some of these to 'mediate' between the individual and the state, to provide a social mechanism through which individuals are brought into mutual association, and their demands and interests made coherent and articulate and brought to bear on political affairs and governmental policies.

Thus, just as we say that power and authority may be diffused throughout a society, so also with consent. In other words, it may be important to ask, when considering the extent to which a government or regime enjoys the consent of the governed, what is the relationship that the members of that society generally have to the major social organizations within which they work and carry on other activities that are of great significance to them? How do they perceive the central systems of social relationships by which their own lives are largely conditioned? Extra-governmental sources may contribute much to the total 'pool of consent' that the society possesses. The diffused willing support on which a government can draw to sustain its authority may be in part a reflection of attitudes and perceptions generated in associations and organizations well below the level of national government. This is, no doubt, a very familiar point as may be seen by remembering the history of the idea of participation. The idea of popular participation in the exercise of political power is clearly connected with the concept of consent, because it would be assumed that men are more likely to consent to a government's exercise of authority when they have had a say in choosing that government, and some say also in the discussion and selection of policies. But it has often also been maintained that popular participation in government at the national level is not likely to be very considerable or effective unless the rank and file of citizens also have opportunities to participate in political activity at a lower level than that of national government—for example, to take part in the activities of trade unions, political parties, local government, and in other smaller organizations or associations which provide a link with the more remote centres of national political authority. This is a type of argument insufficiently taken into account by some who have written about consent. Earlier individualists such as Locke presented the question of consent as if it were almost exclusively one of the direct relationship of individual subjects to government; and this individualistic tradition, in which the individual members of a society directly confront government, and the authority that requires explanation and justification is the authority of government only, has ever since tended to affect the treatment of the doctrine of consent.

What we have to do is to try to define more clearly and fully what is meant by 'consent' when it is claimed that government ought to be based on the consent of the governed, or that democratic states are ones in which the government is supported by a relatively large measure of consent; and then to enquire how it is possible in states as we know them for governments to be founded on consent.

2/The Meaning of Consent

We have tried to suggest the initial question to be attended to if we are to make anything of the notion of government by consent: What is the sense in which it is still significant and important to say that a political order may be supported by the consent of the governed? In this chapter we shall discuss possible meanings of the term 'consent' which may be relevant to this idea. Towards the end of the chapter and in the next we shall examine some of the main issues that arise when we try to apply these meanings to the actual structure and operation of modern states.

It will be useful to begin with two or three preliminary points. Throughout the history of political philosophy, the idea of consent has functioned within a theory of political obligation. Another way of putting this is to say that the conception of the consent of the governed has been proposed as the ground or foundation of right—the right to exercise political authority. For Locke and the classical contract theorists, as for many of his medieval and ancient predecessors, the rightful authority of rulers to rule or exercise authority flowed from the supposed fact that that authority was instituted or exercised by the consent of the governed; that was the ultimate ground of the right to govern. But as the notion of consent came to be embodied in more thorough-going or more fully developed democratic positions, the matter grew somewhat more complex. Throughout the nineteenth century wider sections of the community, in England, France and other Western countries, claimed a share in the exercise of political power, especially through the widening of the franchise. From the point of view of democratic doctrine, it was natural that the notion of government with the consent of the governed should be connected with the central processes of democratic parliamentary government—free elections, adult franchise, and so on.

It is true that in modern democratic ideologies the 'consent of the governed' continued to operate as a justificatory idea indicating a condition under which political authority can be approved. But at the same time, 'consent of the governed' came to acquire a somewhat richer meaning and to express a more stringent demand: it no longer referred merely to the necessary ground of the general right of governments to exercise authority, but also to the processes by which it was thought government should be carried on. As democratic ways of thinking developed, 'consent' came to indicate the role that the governed ought to play in the processes of government, the manner in which citizens ought to be involved directly or indirectly in the activity of governing. So we find contemporary political theorists who seek to clarify the idea of consent writing, not simply about the foundations of the general right to exercise supreme political authority, not about a social contract or any other initial condition by which the right to govern is conferred, but about freedom of speech, freedom to organize, criticize and oppose, about elections and parties, voluntary associations and representative government—in other words, about continuing processes by which, so it is argued, governments are made perpetually responsive to the ideas and demands of the governed and the requirement of government by the consent of the governed is met. It seems clear that as a result of this elaboration of the concept, 'consent' has taken on a burden of meaning absent from the minds of seventeenth- and eighteenth-century contract theorists.

Of course, Locke's view of the contract and of consent, like that of other early writers, was an unhistorical one. Unhistorical not only in the sense that the original contract and consent never occurred historically, but in the (for us) more important sense that the idea of constant social change and development does not get much attention in Locke's theory of consent. For Locke, consent to the exercise of authority is expressed either explicitly or implicitly by subjects simply continuing to reside within the territories of a government. It is in either case a very general acknowledgement of authority but Locke shows little awareness of consent as a situation or relationship between government and citizens that has to be maintained (if such a thing exists at all) within a society and polity continuously changing, where there is an unbroken succession of problems, demands and 'felt needs'. We cannot think intelligibly about politics unless we place social fluidity or change at the centre of our models (politics being indeed one of the main agencies of change); and any concept of consent is unlikely to have any significant application to modern states unless we conceive it as a process, as a relationship between members of a state and their government that must be constantly renewed and maintained. The view of government as trustee for the governed (with which Locke connected the idea of consent) has only an extremely limited application to modern government and its relation to the citizen body; there may be some aspects of that relationship more or less analogous to trusteeship, but it is a highly complex relationship and for the most part one of a different order.

Thus, Locke and other earlier writers place the concept of consent within a context very different from that in which we must place it: therefore, it had a meaning or 'resonance' very different from that which it has for us. For the theorists of the social contract, and for other political writers in earlier centuries, Nicholas of Cusa, for example, the equal power and freedom that all men possess naturally (or in 'the state of nature') engender the problem of explaining how some men can acquire rightful authority over others. To these writers it seemed that the only way that men, by nature equally powerful and free, could come to be under an obligation to obey political authority was by voluntarily placing themselves under it. This is a cluster of concepts—equal natural power and freedom, voluntary acceptance of the obligation to obey —which modern men would not naturally place in the centre of their understanding of the state, its power and authority. For them, equal power and freedom would be a myth, and the 'involuntary' membership of a state and subordination to its laws is much too obvious and omnipresent to allow them to imagine that any obligation to obey the state and its laws derives from a promise or agreement to obey. They may still want to say that consent on the part of the governed characterizes or should characterize in some sense the exercise of political authority within the state; but it seems clear that that sense will be very different (though there may be some common elements) from that given the concept by earlier, highly individualistic and voluntaristic political philosophers.

Because, with the spread and absorption of democratic ideologies, consent has come to be linked with questions concerning the positive role of the governed in the activity of government, or in short with the doctrine of self-government, in a manner not before possible a contemporary writer would naturally approach the task of 'defining' consent in a different way. For one thing, arguments about the right and justification of political authority attract less interest and attention. Since the majority of citizens of most Western countries have for a long time taken the assumptions and institutions of democracy for granted, questions concerning the justification of democratic political life and governmental authority have not seemed to be particularly open or pressing. In so far as the doctrine of government by the consent of the governed has continued to present itself as a *problem* of political theory, it has been more a political and sociological problem than a philosophical one. That is, the question has not so much been *why* government should be based on the consent of the governed but rather *how* it can be based on their consent, though questions more specific than Locke's have continued to be discussed fitfully. These have chiefly concerned the extent to which consent of the governed should be the criterion of legitimate political authority in relation to other possible criteria such as efficiency, strength and stability or national security. Should the requirement of consent imply that the public ought to approve treaties, or be consulted about decisions of peace and war; should governments normally implement only those policies for which they have obtained a clear mandate? Thus, the working out of the claims of consent in detail in relation to the actual or possible political procedures of modern states may still provoke some argument of a partly philosophical nature; but the high-level generalization that governments should be based on the consent of the governed is installed as one of the rhetorical orthodoxies of democratic ideology (so general that it can be assented to by the apologists of almost any form of modern political regime). If the idea of government by consent has continued to hold the interest of political theorists, it is an interest in the institutional arrangements that are available for making governments more dependent on the consent of their subjects.

For this reason, when contemporary political scientists attempt to spell out the 'meaning' of consent, they will naturally pay closer attention to empirical conditions and processes of politics than did their rationalistic predecessors. They will try to identify within the structure and the processes of the state those things which seem to provide an actual or empirical body for the elusive and ambiguous concept of government by consent.

Let us list some examples of political and social conforming behaviour which may plausibly be said to be connected with the idea of consent. It would be possible to differentiate many such situations but seven examples will suffice to illustrate the variety of situations within which consent of some type or 'grade' might be said to be present.

1 We may begin with acquiescence under duress. A man might say, 'I consented to what he proposed or demanded; I acquiesced in it. I did not register disagreement or opposition, but only because I thought that if I had done so I would probably have suffered in the future some disagreeable consequences.' Willingness to conform to the demands of a powerful leader is sometimes of this kind, or induced in this way. Can this properly be taken as an example or type of consent? Many would deny it. But I think we might hesitantly admit it as a type because a man may be brought round to consenting to something being done, although he dislikes it, by the fear of some sanction or deprivation. He could perhaps have resisted or protested; the feared sanction may in fact be a very mild one (no more, perhaps, than the fear of offending someone who is a friend); but we can say that in the end he consented albeit reluctantly. So we might argue that when a man has the power to withhold consent or express dissent, reluctant or 'forced' consent is still a form of consent. Our hesitation in accepting this argument would increase proportionately with the severity of the feared sanctions.

2 There is the type of consent connected with the manipulation of minds. A man possessing power and authority may so control the information that reaches others, the knowledge of the possible alternatives for action that are available to them and so on, that he can cause them to think what he wants them to think and to will what he wants them to will. This type of situation has often prevailed to one degree or another in the history of political and other sorts of organization. Again it is a situation about which people would disagree. Some would deny that such conforming behaviour is properly to be counted as consent; others would concede that it should rank as consent of a certain sort or level. It seems to meet some at least of the criteria of consent: actors in such a situation may agree with enthusiasm to what is proposed or demanded; no fear of sanctions need help to motivate their conduct.

3 There is the sort of acquiescence that may arise from sheer apathy, indifference or habit. One does not dissent or resist,

nor does one conform because one feels threatened or constrained; one simply acquiesces and obeys—it may be from apathy or inertia, or from the habit of obedience so far as that particular social authority and that area of conduct are concerned and nothing has occurred to disturb the disposition to acquiesce. Perhaps this mode of behaviour would fall within Locke's concept of 'tacit consent'; it is surely exemplified by a great deal of ordinary political and social behaviour. Most of us most of the time are controlled by a strong disposition to 'go along' with political and social demands: perhaps we haven't the energy to dissent, or again perhaps we acquiesce because we are not really much involved and prefer to conserve our time and energy for other things in which we are more interested. There seems no doubt that we go along with much that is decided by our government in this way and for these reasons: we lack serious concern. Equally we acquiesce in many of the characteristics of the existing social structure and in many existing social institutions in the same manner. Is this an example of behaviour that manifests consent? Certainly political authorities will usually be quick to claim that it is a manifestation of consent, but some may want to insist that, even if it is, it is consent on a rather low level as are the two earlier examples.

4   Next, there is traditional behaviour: behaviour characterized by the acceptance or following of established traditions of conduct. There could be much argument about what exactly traditional behaviour is and some maintain it involves the acceptance of an existing tradition of conduct as providing a norm of right conduct. This would distinguish traditional behaviour from behaviour that is simply customary or habitual, in which no suggestion of a norm deserving to be accepted need be present. When Weber speaks of 'traditional authority' as one of the main types of authority he probably has in mind more than custom but also the prescriptive force of tradition. If we adopt this more restricted notion of traditional behaviour then this provides an example of consenting behaviour which takes us beyond the examples so far considered; the motivation of the actor includes a feeling for the 'rightness' of the form of behaviour to which he conforms.

5   We may move beyond the absorption of traditions to the types of conforming behaviour which arise from the processes, some of them unconscious, that sociologists call 'socialization'. We

are thinking here, not so much of accommodation to customs and usages, the formation of habits of behaviour (including habits of obedience), or even the absorption of existing traditions of behaviour, but rather the adoption of a variety of norms and codes of 'right' conduct, the adherence to complex systems of values which affect conduct. We 'internalize' values and norms presented to us in our education and social experience; and to the extent that 'internalization' is accomplished, our obedience to norms and values, and to the institutions and authorities they 'legitimize', is a consenting obedience. We obey and conform because we feel with deep conviction that it is right to do so. This must surely be admitted as a type of consent and we may distinguish it from all the types so far mentioned on the ground that it seems to involve (or does often involve) to a greater degree than they do the element of 'voluntariness' or 'identification' with institutions and authorities. It is a very important type for our purposes because much recent sociological theory places very great weight on the 'internalization' of values as one factor contributing to the cohesiveness of societies and the stability of social systems.

6 None of the situations involving consent so far considered seem to bring in very prominently the element of deliberate choice, decision or action. This element may be involved in some of our examples in different forms and degrees but it is not a central element. We shall pass on now to two examples in which this element is clearly more crucial. Take the case of the man who may be said to have consented to what another has done because he has given him *permission* to do it. If he had the right, power or opportunity to dissuade or prevent (or try to dissuade or prevent) the other but has instead indicated his permission for what he knew the other to intend, clearly he has consented to his action.

Some writers have maintained that, so far as the notion of government by the consent of the governed is concerned, this is the really vital type of consenting situation—the sort of situation that is, in fact, invoked when it is claimed that government must derive its legitimacy from the consent of the governed. My granting of permission, it has been argued, involves me in the responsibility for what the political authority does; if someone governs by my express permission, then I am in an important sense governing myself. This is a sense that obviously connects with theories about a social contract: those who make the contract and set up a political authority grant a permission to that authority to govern on their behalf within the particular terms of the contract.

Obviously, this is a narrower (perhaps a sharper) concept of consent than any of the preceding. Because it requires the granting of a permission, it clearly differs from customary or habitual conformity or obedience, from the mere disposition to acquiesce, and from acceptance of authority and its acts flowing from 'internalized' norms or values. It expresses a degree of deliberate commitment to what is authorized or consented to. Again, it is to be distinguished from simple *approval* of what is done, and from simple *support* for it. It is perfectly intelligible to say of some man's action: 'He did not obtain my consent to do what he did but I approve of what he has done.' Thus, the distinction is clear and well supported by ordinary modes of speech. Nevertheless, when we come to consider the very complex processes and relationships within actual political societies, we will be forced to ask whether a concept of consent that would exclude mere approval of the acts of a political authority—or *post facto* consent to what has already been done —is likely to be a very useful tool of political analysis. In other words, is this a specification of what is to be counted as consent which will carry us very far, in the actual circumstances of modern political societies, in developing an account of what is to be included within the idea of government by the consent of the governed? However, it is important to note that the notion of consent as meaning a granted permission or authorization of political authority and its acts has been historically one of the central ideas of the theory of government by the consent of the governed.

7   We can proceed to restrict still more sharply our criteria for the sort of situation we will accept as manifesting consent. The granted permission just discussed may still be a reluctant permission. I may say: 'I did give him permission to act so but I didn't really approve of it.' Someone with authority to grant or withhold permission may often find himself in this situation. This suggests that there is the kind of situation in which I not only give permission to someone to act in a particular manner but positively will that he should do so; I will what he wills. On my part the permission is not qualified, my consent is suffused by the desire that the other should do what he proposes to do. We might describe this as being a very 'strong' concept of consent. And this

'strong' concept also has played a part in the history of theories of government by the consent of the governed. For example, the more radical types of democrat, the exponents of what is sometimes called 'direct democracy', have often asserted or assumed that government by the consent of the governed occurs only when the government gives effect to the already declared will of the governed. Those who have held that government by the consent of the governed requires the institutional devices of referendum and initiative (arrangements whereby the governed are given the opportunity to express their opinion about a measure a government proposes to enact, or are able to propose measures they wish the government to carry out) have tended, at least implicitly, to push the concept of consent towards the 'expression of will' boundary. Or we might say that Rousseau, and the English idealists Green and Bosanquet, were in their own way concerned to elaborate a conception of government by consent (or self-government). The doctrine that the state or political authority when it is truly itself expresses the 'general will' or the 'real will' of citizens tends to amalgamate 'consenting' with 'willing'. But these idealist doctrines with their very special concept of will move far away from common sense notions of consent and its possible meanings.

These, then, are some examples of different sorts of situation or relationship in which it may be said that consent is manifested. No doubt more could be differentiated. One point that has been suggested in several places during our differentiation and comparison of these several types of situation is that these different types of situation might be arranged very crudely along a scale or continuum: in setting them out we seemed in a vague sort of way to be moving from 'weaker' or 'lower level' forms of consent to ones that are 'stronger' or on a 'higher level'. One of the criteria by reference to which this crude continuum seemed to emerge was that of the degree to which deliberate or voluntary decision on the part of those who are conforming or obeying seemed to be involved in the consenting situation. In the argument that follows we shall refer from time to time to the notion of a continuum but we should not wish to press the suggestion very hard. There are many difficulties inherent in any attempt to arrange types of consent along a scale: one of them is the complexity of the notion of 'voluntary' or 'deliberate' action.

We now have to consider the following questions. Which of these different relationships, situations, meanings of consent, shall we admit when we come to identify governments which can be said to govern with the consent of the governed? To which of these situations or meanings do we appeal, or should we appeal, when we want to say that some governments, but not all, are governments whose authority rests on the consent of the governed?

One thing that is clear is that the meaning of consent, as it is used by political writers, oscillates, now taking in a wider span of reference, now a narrower. According to Professor Crick, '. . . *all* industrial and industrialising states are democracies, whether they allow free politics or not: they all depend on the consent of the majority, as peasant cultures never did, and most of them need the actual enthusiasm of the new class of skilled manual workers'.[1] We could truly say that all industrial states depend on the consent of the majority only if we are willing to count as consent attitudes or relationships included within our first four divisions, and if approval as such also counts. Certainly, if we were to insist that consent means and means only prior permission, then Crick's assertion would obviously be false. Professor Plamenatz, on the other hand, in his book *Consent, Freedom and Political Obligation*, specifies the meaning of consent in these ways: 'We have consent whenever the right of one man to act in a certain way is conditional upon another man's having expressed the wish that he should act in that way.' (p. 4). 'Before B can be said to be acting with A's consent, in the sense of the word relevant in this present discussion, A as well as B must be responsible for B's action, so that it can be truly said of the latter that he is acting with the former's permission.' (pp. 15–16). And again, consent is defined as being '. . . an expression of a wish by one man that another should act in a certain way, known and intended to create or increase in the latter the right to act in this way'. (p. 15).[2] Plamenatz explains that he is taking it to be true that government by the consent of the governed is responsible government and that he is seeking the definition of consent necessary if responsible government and government with the consent of the governed are to coincide. Other writers again, taking like Plamenatz the stronger or more restricted view of the meaning of consent, have, unlike him, then concluded that government with the consent of the governed is an 'impossible' notion.[3]

Our task is to determine whether there is a sense of consent according to which it is true to say that some states are governed with the consent of the governed and others are not. It may be true that, if we count as consent virtually the whole spectrum we have set out, then as Crick says 'all industrial and industrialising states depend on the consent of the majority . . .' But political ideologists who, like John Wildman, have claimed that 'all government is in the free consent of the people', and later political theorists who have tried to connect political freedom and democracy with a particular way of organizing and exercising political authority, namely, with the existence of consent as the 'basis' of political authority, have clearly not been arguing for a position such as Professor Crick's.

In the following discussion we shall not try to 'lay down' a meaning that consent ought to have. We shall instead consider some of the characteristics of states (necessarily at a very general or abstract level) with a view to identifying what processes and relationships within those states may reasonably be regarded as expressing consent.

If we consider states as they are, we find that *all* of the different attitudes or relationships we distinguished are present. All are important elements in the political and social system. There is more or less unreflective conformity to habit and custom; acquiescence and obedience arising from apathy, indifference or ignorance; conformity or even active support for social authorities and their ways which is the product of successful 'socialization'; obedience secured by sanctions or the expectation that sanctions may be incurred; permission granted in advance (either explicitly or by imputation) for the measures taken by political authority; the willing of particular actions to be taken by political authority. All of these, in any state, form part of the constitution of political conformity or obedience: they are all psychological and sociological constituents of effective political authority.

We may add one or two further obvious remarks about them. The social and political behaviour of every member of a society is affected or determined by all of these relationships with respect to the different aspects of the social and political systems: in the activities of everyone there are exemplifications of each of them. But they are 'mixed' in different ways in the social personalities of individuals. Some of us are more constantly creatures of custom, some more successfully 'socialized', some more apathetic, uninterested or ignorant concerning social and political affairs, some more active 'willers' in political and social matters. And, to the extent that it is possible to characterize intelligibly political societies as a whole, we may say also that these several attitudes, relationships, modes of behaviour are present in different 'mixes' and are distributed differently in different societies. This is perhaps the basic point for our further discussion of consent. It would be impossible to imagine a complex and stable political system in which all these modes of political behaviour were not operative.

Now, if we take the case in which the citizen wills the existence of a particular political authority, or the action it takes, we may certainly say that to the extent this situation occurs the political system manifests consent of the governed. It is assumed that we may agree that a Rousseau-type society (leaving aside all the obscurities and problems of the notion of the general will) would be a society to a very large degree expressive of the consent of its members; so also with any association so small that its officers can ascertain and carry out the wishes of members.

But if we propose to allow nothing except this to count as consent, then no society will manifest consent except in a very minor degree. This is not to say that there may not be important differences of degree between different societies; nevertheless, in *any* society there is very little within the complex institutional structure of political authority, and only a small part of what political authorities enact or perform, that can be said to be expressive of the antecedent will of the governed. Moreover, it is probably true that it is only a very small proportion of any political community that enters into this kind of relation with a government. It can be identified as present more often at some levels of political life than at others: if we were seeking examples, we would more easily find them in relation to particular pieces of legislation than in relation to features of the constitutional structure of the political system.

We have just said that this form of consent admits of differences of degree. (This is an intelligible notion but a very difficult one to deal with theoretically because the quantitative differences we have in mind would have to be measured on several different dimensions.) Therefore it is not difficult to suggest ways in which it could be expanded. The advocates of such political devices as 'initiative' and 'referendum' have had this objective in mind. Nevertheless, for reasons connected with very familiar conditions under which modern, large-scale states work, it would be unrealistic to suppose that a relatively large part of an established political system, or of the processes of policy making and implementation, could be subject to consent in this sense.[4] Thus, if only this counts as consent, we will find no modern complex society which is characterized by a considerable degree of consent by the governed to governmental authority and activity—but it is worth again emphasizing that differences between different states are relevant and important.

Let us move to another position on our spectrum: the case in which we may say that permission has been granted in advance for the exercise of authority or for particular acts of authority such as policy decisions, legislative acts and administrative arrangements. This can properly be treated as a form of consent, and in the modern state it is a very important one. Modern elections with the presentation of alternative candidates and programmes involve in some ways and to some extent this process of granting permission, although as students of elections have demonstrated abundantly there is much more involved in an election than simple democratic ideology would suggest. More recent writers on the theory of consent have tended to take the electoral process as being the institutional centre of government by consent. There are other important forms as well. In his *Public Opinion and American Democracy*, V. O. Key speaks of different forms of consensus: 'supportive', 'permissive' and 'decisive'. 'Permissive consensus' refers to the process whereby public opinion is prepared for policies and measures governments are in due course enabled or encouraged to embark on. No one will doubt that this is consent, and also that it is a form or process of consent that has an important role in many of the states we classify as democratic.

This type of consent also exists in different forms and degrees in different societies. And again these differences are measured along different dimensions: we might consider as relevant such variables as the numbers involved in a 'permissive consensus', the frequency with which governmental action is backed by it, the range and variety of matters of general public interest in relation to which it occurs. We can easily point to factors which may be present or absent within a particular society which affect the strength and degree to which permission in this sense is present: political organizations, voluntary associations, active, diverse and independent organs of opinion, the level of education, the condition of civil liberties, and so on.

So far things seem fairly clear. But difficulties arise when we consider states of acquiescence and of approval, and it is immediately obvious that each of these terms refers in ordinary practice to a range of different attitudes, relationships or processes. To take the most obvious distinction, acquiescence may be forced and grudging compliance or it may be enthusiastic willingness to go along with some proposal. Because of the range of attitudes that may be classed as states of acquiescence and approval there are problems concerning their connection with consent.

Some writers have firmly distinguished approval from consent, a view taken by Plamenatz in the original edition of his *Consent, Freedom and Political Obligation*. We have already conceded that one may approve of an action to which one did not grant consent. This is possible when consent is taken to be prior permission. However, we now must ask whether the identification of consent with the granting of a permission is an unreasonably narrow specification for the purposes of locating consent in the actual processes of government. Plamenatz himself, as we have noted, came round to that view and discusses a sense in which consent does not involve in any literal sense the granting of a permission—the taking part in an established process of free election. We shall not for the present consider this case but press the concession Plamenatz makes a little further.

We frequently talk about governments or political leaders or élites as manufacturing consent. Only the most naïve now entertain the model of a political system in which policy initiatives proceed from the body of the citizens and the function of government is to give effect to the popular will. For a great number of empirical reasons we recognize that the politics of complex societies cannot work like that; that political parties and other organizations, leaders and élites, bureaucracies and governments necessarily assume such functions as selecting and defining issues or problems, assembling and distributing information, proposing policies and advocating them, engaging in public persuasion, demonstrating the satisfactoriness of general lines of policy by initiating practical measures that are seen to work. According to most established current views concerning the nature of political systems and government, these are among the indispensable roles of leadership and government. These are among the ways in which governments (and other influential political organizations and groups) may forge, consolidate and expand the approval or support which enables them to continue to enjoy and deploy authority—or, as we commonly say, manufacture consent. It would seem to be a dubious taxonomy of relationships which would refuse to accept these processes as possibly genuine (there are qualifications yet to be mentioned) instances of consent.

The familiar situation we have just pointed to would fall within Professor Key's 'supportive consensus'. But that would also include another situation equally important although different. The areas of social affairs in relation to which a government is innovating or producing a flow of new measures are small in comparison with the whole extent of the area of administration with which a government is concerned. Its innovatory policies are carried out within the wider context of established and settled policies and administrative routines. The widespread approval or acceptance of these passive areas of policy are equally the conditions of the more or less untroubled exercise of political authority. And it may therefore be argued that this is also a sense in which a successful government depends upon the consent of the governed, however bitterly it may be opposed and criticized on specific issues. The consent in such a case may often be part of a consensus: that is, both parties within a two-party parliamentary system may when in office uphold and administer much the same set of settled policies. This, then, is one part of the 'supportive consensus' of a political system which may be counted as an example of consent.

But there are difficulties about taking these things as expressions of consent. What evidence can be adduced for the approval and consent that is claimed in such cases? What are indicia or criteria of consent? And those who put these questions may answer that (at any rate, in systems of representative, parliamentary democracy) the public expresses approval or consent by means of the institution of free elections; an electorate authorizes, so to speak, what a government in office has done or withdraws its consent to a continuation of authority along similar lines. This view brings the concept of consent back closer to the idea of a manifest act of permission or authorization. Thus, some contemporary writers place free elections and representative government at the institutional centre of a system of government by the consent of the governed; Professor Plamenatz, for example, and Professor Gewirth.[5]

It would not be satisfactory to treat elections as if they had a quite special significance in the total process of enlisting or expressing consent. Elections themselves are complex and equivocal in their nature or function: the very large amount of 'traditional' or 'habitual' voting (voting in accordance with family, occupational, class or ethnic tradition) shows that for many voting can be as much a matter of following custom or codes absorbed through the processes of 'socialization' as other forms of behaviour are. And within the political system elections and election campaigns cannot be separated from all the other ways in which citizens react to and bring pressure to bear on governments and they in their turn head off or conciliate opposition. Since the business of forging consent and seeking endorsement for continued authority continues all the time, it would be sociologically unrealistic to attribute to elections a unique function within a system of government by consent, although the formal constitutions of parliamentary democracies do attribute to them a special legal authority.[6]

There are, however, other difficulties about allowing 'supportive' consent to count as the consent which those who have advocated the idea of government by the consent of the governed have had in mind. This kind of approval or support can be of many different kinds. We have emphasized that the advocates of government by consent of the governed are reaching after a form of consent which will differentiate political systems which are free or democratic from those that are not. But it is obvious that the kind of support and approval we have been describing can be manifest to a very high degree within states that are distinctly authoritarian and 'totalitarian'. Such governments can also be skilful in conciliating opposition and forging consent; consent in this sense can be manipulated by such means as incessant propaganda, lying and censorship. Despots have ruled peasant societies which have been inert and dominated by custom and superstition. Perhaps it could even be claimed that such rulers have ruled with the approval of their subjects—at least there may have been little sense of oppression. For reasons of this kind, it seems clear that we cannot, without further specification, conclude that 'supportive' acquiescence or approval may count as consent.

Clearly, to accommodate this line of argument we need additional criteria. Among societies in all of which there is a very large measure of acquiescence with, even approval of, established political authority and its policies, we can distinguish (very roughly and broadly at least) degrees of passivity and activity. We can distinguish popular or very widespread support which is unreflecting or apathetic or no more than a manifestation of long-established habits of obedience and conformity from support which manifests itself in enthusiastic approval of the policies or declared objectives of a regime. And we will be inclined to say that as we move from the one towards the other we are approaching the pole of consent. But even this still does not take into account all or nearly all of the criteria that we normally take to be relevant in estimating the presence or absence of consent. The vast mass meetings which listened to Hitler in Nuremberg did not seem to be lacking in passionate approval of his assertions and his policies. It would be impossible to say (in accordance with our ordinary understanding of the meaning of the word) that these meetings were *not* expressing consent to the authority of the Führer; but we might also say that other things commonly connected with the relationship of consent are lacking. To what extent is this enthusiastic approval generated by propaganda which operates free from any countervailing influences? To what extent are these people insulated from alternative or dissenting opinions and policies? To what extent, therefore, are they ignorant of the nature and significance of the beliefs and policies they applaud, and of the nature of the alternatives; and lack as a further consequence the possibilities of decision and choice? To what extent, then, are policies fashioned for them and imposed upon them, instead of being policies which in some measure arise from their own needs, situation and initiative?

These considerations are so obvious and familiar that it is unnecessary to spend time on them. They indicate, however, the further dimensions of consent as that concept comes to be further elaborated. The general position that our analysis has suggested is that there are weaker and stronger, more passive and more active, senses and forms of consent. The more active forms, of course, increasingly bring in the elements of deliberation, choice, decision, permission and initiative. These different forms can easily if roughly be set out schematically on a conceptual continuum. But historically, as the concept of consent was continuously developed as a key element of democratic theories and ideologies, the elements of deliberation, decision and initiative have naturally been progressively emphasized and consent has come to be regarded as specifying the nature or the *raison d'être* of the whole system of familiar democratic parliamentary institutions. Thus, consent has come to be viewed, not as an original act or series of discrete and repeated acts, but as a continuous process of interaction between the governed and the government by means of which governments become relatively more responsive to the interests, demands and initiatives of their subjects. And when the implications or necessary conditions of these relationships of interaction and responsiveness are spelt out, they are seen to include civil liberties, freedom of speech and organization, political parties, the existence of a variety of separate and independent sources of political energy and enterprise, elections and representative government: in short, the processes of consent tend to coincide in the end with almost the whole of the mechanism of liberal parliamentary democracy.

We have spoken of a continuum of meanings or forms of consent. The question may still be pressed: Which of the separate relationships or situations distinguished on this continuum *really* counts as consent? This, I would argue, is an unfruitful question. It would be easy to establish a meaning of consent by fiat: to say, for example, that the governed may be said to consent only where they have authorized by express act the exercise of authority by a particular government or expressly granted permission for a particular policy; or again, to declare that the governed are to be said to consent wherever they acquiesce in the government's exercise of authority without expressed dissent or opposition. But there are various reasons why this is a pointless procedure. The several sorts of relationship we have been examining flow into their neighbours by gradations that make clear demarcation impossible. Though Cassinelli says that consent implies voluntariness while the relation of members to the state is clearly involuntary, we can easily see that the dichotomy between the voluntary and the involuntary is incapable of illuminating a great area of social and political behaviour, and to what is probably the greater part of political behaviour neither the concept of the voluntary nor of the involuntary clearly applies. Who can say that the habitual, frictionless but unreflecting following of customary political routines is either voluntary or involuntary? These are segments of political and social behaviour where the categories of the voluntary and the involuntary are unworkable and unilluminating.

Second, as already stressed, the structure of any more or less stable system of political authority depends heavily upon most of the relationships present in our continuum. The element of deliberation, choice between alternatives, the exercise of initiative, its expression in contested elections and representative governments, responsiveness by government to pressures and initiatives of the governed—these are dimensions of consent that may be relatively prominent in some political systems and virtually absent in others. But other dimensions are probably not only essential but very substantial parts of any political system. If we consider not only the assent that may be accorded a government, and not only the approval and support of its policies or legislation but also the acceptance of the general political or constitutional system by which authority is defined and constituted, then it seems certainly true as a matter of empirical fact that the support that most members of most states most of the time give to this part of the polity is 'involuntary'—not forced or imposed but the unreflecting adherence to the customary or familiar.

Now, it is difficult to say: 'This is true, but these relationships and modes of behaviour are irrelevant because they fall outside what we are thinking of as the domain within which the concepts of consent and absence of consent apply.' As a matter of political sociology, these areas or modes of behaviour *do* form part of the system of consent on which a political authority may depend: the authority that a party may gain from an election depends in part on the strength of the popular adherence to basic constitutional practices and conventions—and this is never more true than when in mid-term the policies of a government are encountering bitter and widespread opposition. This is, perhaps, the chief reason why it is arbitrary and misleading to try to separate sharply the different 'gradations' of consent. A concept of consent which enables us to emphasize these relationships and continuities will both render the sociological facts more accurately and pose the philosophical questions in a more adequate context.

Does it then follow—if we stress the continuities—that all industrial states, as Crick says, depend on the consent of the majority? (Bringing in the majority introduces questions which we have not and need not yet worry about.) It is very hard to imagine a functioning state in which various areas or sectors of the polity and the social system are not maintained by or with the consent of considerable portions of the population, and it is possible that an authority in a modern complex society could not continue to rule without a large measure of consent. But our analysis suggests that this is not a very informative or significant assertion. The more interesting question is: What, in any given society, are the prevailing and predominant forms of consent and their distribution? To understand the character of a society so far as government by consent or its absence is concerned, we have to concern ourselves with the anatomy of consent. Even within one society we will find different forms or gradations of consent differently distributed in different sections of the citizen body and in relation to different aspects of the political system and of governmental policy or administration. Within one population are different constellations of the attitudes, relationships and modes of behaviour relevant to the qualitative and quantitative estimation of the mode and measure in which the government may be said to be based on the consent of the governed. And, at least theoretically, it is possible to compare different societies by the application of the same categories and the same scales, though the practical questions of identification of modes, measuring and scaling are another matter. At any rate, in a broad and partly intuitive way we can, and as a matter of course do, rank societies in relation to one another as regards the presence/absence of consent in its several different forms.

Of course, those who maintain that liberal democratic states are examples of government by consent while authoritarian or dictatorial regimes are not, are, often tacitly, applying a particular set of criteria to which they allot a special weight. They are especially concerned with those forms of consent that come high on our spectrum: those that involve such features as governmental responsiveness and public initiative, the free availability of alternative governments and policies, and the consequent presence of deliberation, decision, choice and the explicit authorization of authority and policy. In so far as they include in their concept of consent wide popular acquiescence in established institutions and forms and procedures of government, what will concern them will be such questions as the extent to which this acquiescence is widely shared and is unforced. It is by putting the weight on such variables as these that the notion of government by consent serves to differentiate (at least as a matter of degree) between different types of regime. Similarly, when writers speak of maximizing consent within a state, it is the accentuation of these characteristics of the political system that they usually have in mind. And if a philosopher were now to assert that only those political authorities which rest on the consent of the governed can rightly demand obedience, it may well be that what he is claiming is that only those forms of government which admit in large measure of the relationships or processes mentioned earlier in this paragraph are morally justifiable. (Of course, we would still expect him to explain in greater

3/The Anatomy of Consent

So far we have tried only to indicate roughly the modes of behaviour and attitudes that are familiar examples of consenting behaviour. In this chapter we will say something about the ways in which consent typically manifests itself in democratic societies of the Western type, and about some of the problems connected with the securing of the consent of the governed.

This is a difficult subject which can here be dealt with only fragmentarily and in very general terms. Obviously, the enormous complexity of modern societies makes it impossible to generalize profitably about the extent to which they are based on the consent of their members. Because of the great complexity of attitudes, motivations, beliefs and relationships that characterize individuals and social groups, it is not easy to know that we have identified them correctly or correctly judged their qualities. And, as we saw, the attitudes and modes of behaviour that may be associated with consent shade into one another. It is therefore never easy to know how to interpret the behaviour and attitudes of social groups in spite of the labours of recent political scientists and sociologists.

We shall speak from time to time of the 'distribution' of consent within a society. The purely theoretical notion of a pattern which represents the manner in which apathy, indifference, forced compliance, consent or dissent are distributed is perhaps intelligible, but of course it is another matter to attempt to describe their *actual* distribution within society. Apart from the manner in which different attitudes are interwoven in individuals there is the problem that the same individuals and groups are related differently, and respond differently, to different aspects of society, or to different policies of a government. As often as not it is simply false or unilluminating to say of a group either that it consents or does not consent to the government. Further, the distribution pattern of consent is largely very unstable and in continuous flux. The attitudes and motives that concern us are transmuted and redistributed as new problems present themselves, as the 'state of the nation' changes, as new policies take effect. These are some of the problems that we confront if we try to talk about consent (or the consent of the governed) as an empirical state of affairs. Political philosophers who have confined themselves to formulating the 'principles' that define 'government by the consent of the governed' ignore the empirical difficulties and produce breath-taking over-simplifications. But in spite of these discouraging preliminary reflections, we will try to say something about typical forms and distributions of consent in Western-type democracies and about the institutional problems of attempting to apply concepts of consent to actual political practice.

Instability, of course, is not everywhere. There is a considerable degree of stability and continuity in group attitudes of compliance, consent, dissent and opposition. Without it an orderly, organized political system could not operate at all: political parties, governments and other organizations must be able to anticipate regularity in modes of response to particular types of situations and policies if they are to be able to function. During the last century and more Western governments have been able to anticipate confidently that when they declare war their subjects will fight it; when they impose taxes, citizens will pay them; and, negatively, if they were to introduce industrial conscription or internal passports they would in all probability encounter a considerable volume of dissent and opposition. Among sociologists, consensus theorists have been especially interested in exploring these more basic stabilities and continuities of belief and attitude; but the controversies within the discipline about whether these stabilities are really evidence for the existence of consensus is another illustration of the difficulty of interpreting the attitudes or motivations that are associated with observable modes of behaviour.

It will be useful to repeat here a point already made. I asserted that it is more fruitful to include within the concept of consent the whole continuum of attitudes, motivations and relationships which can be classified, without linguistic impropriety, as forms of consent. And it seems to me that we cannot speak about the actual distribution and operation of consent within a state (including democratic states) in any illuminating way unless we include all these different forms or 'grades' of consent. The main reason I gave for this catholicity (though, as I noted, it is rejected by some political philosophers) was that these different forms of consent in practice interpenetrate and interact with one another within individuals and within groups, and one cannot understand consent as something that affects political authority unless one takes account of this interaction. At this point there are two broad types of distinction to be made. There are the different forms or 'grades' of consent. Also, there are the different 'areas' or 'levels' of social organization and activity in relation to which we may say consent is given or withheld. Examples of this are aspects of the wider social system such as the distribution of property or the established ways in which economic production is organized and controlled; access to education and to other social goods and services; the broad constitutional structure of political authority; the particular government holding power at the moment; the policies of that government. These are chosen at random to show what is meant by 'areas' or 'levels' of social organization and activity which may win consent or provoke dissent and one of the main themes of this chapter will be that the volume and quality of consent that is manifest in the political areas will usually be strongly affected by attitudes that prevail in other areas or levels of social organization. This, of course, is the stalest commonplace of political sociology: it has to be stated here to emphasize that the concept of consent will be fairly useless in throwing light on the structure and working of political societies unless we understand the concept in a wider rather than narrower fashion.

Political philosophers, pursuing their traditional interest in the idea of consent as a criterion of political obligation—as defining the conditions under which governments rightfully claim authority or citizens are under an obligation to obey—have given some recognition to these different interpenetrating areas. Sometimes they have raised the question to *what* must consent be given if we are to say that government is based on the consent of the governed. Is it required, for example, that citizens (or a majority of them) consent to the broad set of constitutional rules or arrangements by which political authority is constituted or defined? Is it meant that they must consent to the particular government in office (as many assume they do when governments are chosen in the democratic manner by free elections)? Is there no government by consent unless electors approve of a government's specific policies?[1]

It would seem at first sight that 'consent of the governed' ought to include consent to, or unforced acceptance of, the basic rules and arrangements whereby a government acquires the legal right to govern. People will not usually consent to the exercise of power which has been established by methods they reject—if they can protest. But, while we must look at this level of political life in an examination of the anatomy of consent, by the same reasoning we ought to extend it to take in a much wider area still of basic institutions and established social relationships and functions. We have to move outside the area of the strictly political. It is true, of course, that theories of consent originated as theories of political authority and the basis of political obedience, and it is natural that they have focused on political institutions and processes. But the whole point of modern political sociology has been to grade the ways in which states and other structures of political power are affected by the environment of social attitudes and relationships. As we shall briefly note the intensity, quality and distribution of political consent are connected with attitudes and behaviour that prevail in many other sectors of the social system.*

Let us begin with some remarks about the constitutional rules and procedures (taking 'constitutional' in a fairly broad sense) that regulate the 'distribution and exercise of power'. In what sense can it be said that, within Western-type democracies, these are based on the consent of the governed? And in what sense consistent with clear political and social necessities could consent be required or desired?

The histories of different Western democracies suggest different answers to the first question. At different times in the history of the same country one might give different answers. In some countries, for example France of the Third Republic and Weimar Germany, there has been a relatively high level of dissent from the established constitutional regime; active and powerful forces have wished for a different constitutional structure. And even in those stable democracies in which there has not been much apparent dissent from the established constitutional order for a very long time—Britain, the United States, the 'older' British dominions, Scandinavian countries—on occasion some feature of the constitutional system has become an active political issue. In Britain, the controversies of 1910–11 concerning the powers of the House

---

* As Bendix and Lipset put it: 'Political science starts with a state and asks how it affects society, while political sociology starts with a society and asks how it affects the state, i.e. the formal institutions for the distribution and exercise of power.' ("Political Sociology", in *Current Sociology*, vi, 1957.)

of Lords are an example; in the United States, Roosevelt's proposal to add to the judges of the Supreme Court is another.

There is another type of situation worth noting in this connection, that in which some part of the established constitutional rules and processes are not accepted by part of the community and where a minority's breach of the rules in question is tolerated. The United States has provided some interesting examples of this sort. Thus, for a long time the use in some American states of such devices as literacy tests, poll taxes and other means of discouraging Negroes from exercising their constitutional right to vote was tolerated. It is probably true that in all states, however stable politically they may be, there always exists some opposition to (and not infrequently some evasion or defiance of) some parts of the constitutional rules.

Provided, however, that there are no bitter and unresolved conflicts within the social order the available evidence suggests that the bulk of the community is not much concerned with the basic organization of political authority. And even where issues concerning the structure of authority do appear to be divisive and there is strong support and strong dissent, it seems to be a comparatively small group of political activists and sophisticates who manifest definite beliefs and attitudes toward issues of this sort.* The great majority of members of a modern parliamentary democracy probably conform to the basic rules and procedures—the competitive party system, elections, representation, party parliamentary government and so on—in a manner closely analogous to customary or habitual behaviour. It is, however, unlikely that many citizens conform primarily because of a consciously held set of political beliefs and values. On the contrary, it seems more plausible that going through constitutionally prescribed arrangements is more in the nature of abiding to the custom of the country. The same would apply to acceptance of the results of the procedures, e.g. the assumption of power by the party successful in a

* In Australia, which has a written federal constitution and where proposed constitutional amendments go to a popular referendum and must be approved by a majority of electors voting in a majority of the six states, only a very small minority of proposed amendments has secured the necessary majority, even in those cases where both major political parties have supported the amendment and tried to persuade the electorate of the political, economic, etc., advantages of it. Political students are inclined to think that part of the invariably large 'No' vote corresponds to the 'don't knows' of the public opinion polls.

general election. And at least in a high proportion of the established Western-type democracies, it requires a quite drastic disturbance of the economy or some other aspect of familiar social patterns to cause the solid core of the community to review its habitual acceptance of the basic organization of political authority.

We are speaking of most of the citizens. This is not necessarily true of a small body of political leaders, professionals, political intellectuals and administrators. They may be a very important factor in sustaining constitutional stability and some political sociologists believe that, although there usually does not exist anything to be called a popular consensus that supports the constitutional order, that order may, however, require a consensus among the political and administrative 'élite'.

If something like this is true in a stable democracy, then the type of consent typically found at this level is identical with, or very close to, shared habitual participation in established modes of behaviour. C. J. Friedrich has argued that this is what the so-called consensus of many sociologists in fact is: not a general, shared acceptance of values, principles or norms, but common participation in established and familiar forms of action or patterns of behaviour.[2] No doubt, there is much force in this so far as acceptance of the basic structure of political authority in a community is concerned. It is an occupational hazard of political philosophers and other intellectuals to assume that ordinary men would not act as they do unless they possessed sets of values, principles and rules to tell them how to act. There is always the temptation to overlook the possibility that we act as we do much of the time simply because we observe from our earliest years that this is how men always seem to act in this sort of situation.

But having asserted this to be the central fact in the economically advanced Western democracies, we can admit without inconsistency that other, less decisive, features are also present. In any society in which democratic procedures have been long established most citizens will probably have some feeling for the ethos of democratic institutions. It would be surprising if the powerful instruments of 'socialization' which modern democracies command—including universal and highly uniform systems of public education—have not had some success in implanting the symbols, sentiments and attitudes of democracy. But even this is subject to many qualifications. For one thing, it seems that the better educated, the more articulate, those who occupy more 'responsible' positions in the operation of social institutions of all kinds, and those who gain more of the fruits of highly industrialized society, will tend to have absorbed more of the ethos of the system than others. A number of American political studies have suggested that there can be a great deal of inconsistency between the high-level political generalities people will endorse when asked by a pollster and the concrete measures they would approve or endorse in particular cases.[3]

Again, in the area of political behaviour many people subscribe to double or multiple moralities: many trade unionists, for example, support forms of organization and procedure in trade unions which they would strongly oppose if applied within the state (where they feel themselves vulnerable). Also, of course, the lack of congruence between the principles and assumptions that apply to the organization and exercise of political authority and those applying to the government of industry produces tensions and ambiguities of attitude. Or we might examine the interesting way in which the orthodox constitutional principles and moralities are supplemented and qualified by other practices which, though they conflict with the orthodoxies, command a great deal of popular approval. The politics of the United States provide many examples: e.g. the working of the political caucuses and machines and assorted forms of bribery and reward, such as providing jobs and contracts to mobilize support. (Merton has argued that these devices serve the purpose of an informal system of social welfare.[4]) It is not difficult to see that the pattern of consent that supports the constitutional framework of a stably working democratic system is woven from a multitude of threads.

Nor could one ignore Weber's 'traditional' forms of legitimacy. In so-called 'traditional' societies not only the person of the rulers but also the rules, rituals and procedures by means of which their authority is acquired, symbolized and exercised, draw emotional support from religion, tradition or custom that have their roots in more primordial forms of social organization. These attitudes and motivations have become very faint indeed in the secularized, industrialized and democratized Western societies. Yet, in Britain, the coincidence of political authority with social prestige and eminence, which survived long after the opening of the period of democratization, meant that popular assent to the whole structure of authority was supported by the 'ceremonial' aspects of the constitution and the well of social 'deference' of which Bagehot wrote

Even in the United States a cult of 'the constitution' was promoted with some success, even though there is no democratic polity in the world in which the formal and officially promulgated constitution has been so extensively modified and abrogated in many of its parts by popularly supported forms of organization and procedures and by tolerated evasions and defiances.

Perhaps these remarks serve no other purpose than to illustrate the complexity of the topic. However, we will stick to our central assertion that the chief form of consent which supports the basic structure of political authority in a Western-type democracy is the form of acquiescence which closely resembles habitual or customary following of established practice. This kind of acquiescence, of course, falls very low down on our continuum of consent and perhaps most political theorists would deny that it should count as consent at all. Professor Gewirth, who distinguished 'the method of consent' which he believes to be implied by the doctrine of 'government based on the consent of the governed' from the '*generic dispositional* version of the consent principle', which views consent as a 'long range habit or custom of obedience', would probably exclude it. But his exposition leaves some difficulties. He argues that 'Government by consent means that the specific holders of political authority are not independent variables so far as their authority is concerned but are dependent on the votes of the electorate.' He also says that 'the consent which is a necessary condition of political obligation . . . is rather the maintenance of a method which leaves open to every sane, non-criminal adult the opportunity to discuss, criticise and vote for or against the government'.[5]

At this late point in his argument, Gewirth is clearly thinking only of the choice and the authority of a particular government within an established democratic polity. But he said earlier that 'the real question for consent theory involves . . . what kind of government there should be, who should have the authority to govern. The question of political obligation to which consent provides the answer is not, Why should one obey any government at all? but rather, Which government should one obey?' (pp. 135–6). The question, What kind of government should there be? suggests that in the consent theory consent should also apply to those constitutional arrangements which determine in part what kind of government there is. Thus, we may ask, does the theory of consent require that 'every sane, non-criminal adult' must have the opportunity 'to discuss, criticise and vote for or against' the constitution?

One must assume that the answer would be 'Yes'. And one might add that in democratic countries men do have the opportunity to criticize and vote for or against the constitution in whole or in part: therefore, the fundamental arrangements by which political authority is constituted are also subject to the 'method of consent'. But this would surely be a strained and unconvincing interpretation of the nature or anatomy of consent in democratic communities. Gewirth's theory of consent seems plausible enough in relation to ordinary democratic political activity. There is a continuous public competition between competing parties, pressure groups, organs of opinion, policies and recommendations. Electors, no doubt, are either constantly expressing preferences or at least appear to have constant, immediate and perhaps readily utilizable opportunities to do so. This is not, however, normally the case as regards the important elements within the constitutional structure. Though there are usually small dissident groups which are known to prefer some other way of establishing political power (Communist groups, for example), they are rarely able to make significant issues of more general matters concerning the organization of power unless acute economic or other social stress has so shaken established social habit or practice as to enable the basic political structure to be called into question. Indeed, Communist and other anti-democratic movements, when economic and social conditions are relatively undisturbed, do not as a rule emphasize the fundamental arrangements for the allocation of power but themselves conform, working within the system of party politics and parliamentary government.

This is not to say that there are not in all countries many features of fundamental political arrangements and processes that might not well be raised and debated and many of them *are* debated by constitutional and political theorists. One such issue concerns the structure and modes of procedure of modern political parties, for example their control of the process of nomination of electoral candidates. But normally such matters do not get raised as public issues: the mass of the democratic public has displayed only the faintest interest in questions of constitutional and political machinery. Partly for this reason, it is a very 'low' order of consent (in terms of our scale and Gewirth's own definition of consent) which constitutes the foundation of support for the most general forms of procedure and processes of government; not forgetting, however, the very important role of the 'élites' who participate in the management of political and governmental processes and whose attitudes and motivations are probably very different.

Whatever the quality of the consent accorded by most citizens at this level of political organization, it is a necessary condition of the different forms of consent expressed in elections, choices between parties or policies, support for an elected government, and so on, which other writers take to be the true meaning of consent in a state based on the consent of the governed. Unless this 'long range habit or custom of obedience' existed, the other activities and forms of consent would not exist either. We return to the question: In what sense of 'consent' should consent be required or desired at this level of the political system?

We will not attempt a detailed answer, but make only one point. There are obvious reasons why it might be undesirable if central features of the constitutional system were always the subject of questioning; if there were incessant dissent and criticism; the advocacy of alternative proposals; the necessity for the electorate to make decisions or express preferences about questions of this type. We have mentioned that the available evidence suggests that the majority of citizens of modern states are uncomfortable if faced by such questions and for better or worse show a powerful inclination to avoid them. And strong arguments could be mustered to support the conclusion that governments, either democratic or non-democratic, are unlikely to operate very well unless there exists a broad and stable foundation of acquiescence in the basic political arrangements or institutions. Of course, states may be paralyzed when powerful minorities are attacking the basic structures. But far short of this, one would expect that if the machinery by which governments are chosen, constituted and carried on were itself frequently the subject of disputation and decision, this would not enhance the capacity of governments to rule 'with the consent of the governed'.* Thus, it could be that for democracies

---

* Children often spend more time quarrelling about the rules of their game than playing it. Ever since the Revolution France has suffered politically and socially from lack of agreement about central constitutional issues. And the records of the United Nations and other international assemblies and agencies perhaps provide examples of the truth that, where 'procedural' issues can readily be made a subject of contention, the rational consideration of 'substantial' questions is not facilitated; on the contrary, 'procedural' questions arise to block substantial progress.

as well as for authoritarian regimes, habitual acquiescence, or what Key called 'supportive consensus' (at least in the absence of genuine consensus of a more active, conscious and committed kind, which is never in any case likely to be achieved), has a great many virtues or advantages.

So much, then, for this area or level of social organization and behaviour and the kind of consent typically to be found operating there. Let us now say something about other 'areas' within the social and political systems.

The question of the nature of the consent that may be accorded to the more general or basic organization of political authority is not now much considered by political theorists; what is more usually discussed is what it means to say that a government enjoys the consent of the governed. This is really the question Gewirth examines. But speaking still more accurately, consent as such is not very often talked about by contemporary political theorists. In the development of political thinking during the last century and a half the notion of consent has become wholly absorbed into the more general concept of democratic government; and to ask what government by the consent of the governed means has become synonymous with asking what democracy means. Thus, most contemporary political theorists do implicitly what Gewirth explicitly does: 'the method of consent' is identified with the familiar institutions and processes of parliamentary political systems; the theory of consent, if that phrase can still be usefully employed, becomes nothing more than the theory of what a democratic system is.

Of course, what justifies this identification is the conviction that only a Western-type democratic system with its universal franchise, rights of freedom of organization and of speech, freedom to oppose and dissent, competitive parties, representative government responsible to the electorate, is capable of realizing government with the consent of the governed. Thus, the 'method of consent' becomes identical with the political institutions and processes which enable the public to act upon political leaders and governments, and compel governments to secure consent by their responsiveness.

On this view consent is taken to be a continuous process, emerging progressively, or failing to emerge, from the interaction of social movements, public beliefs, interests and demands and, on the other side, the proposals and decisions of parties and governments. The competition between parties for support, for votes and for governmental office, is the central institutional requirement of this 'method of consent'. One of its strengths is that it tries to adapt the concept of consent to the practicalities of actual complex political life.

There are still questions to be asked. Is it true that this is the *only* method by which government with the consent of the governed can be achieved? That is, is the identification of the democratic method and the 'method of consent' legitimate? And is it *a* method of consent? That is, to what extent does the Western-style democratic system achieve consent, and in what ways and forms? It is the second question we have been pursuing in this chapter and we will stay with it.

When we think of a government securing the consent of the governed through responsiveness to public interests and demands, we naturally tend to think first of policies which serve public needs or interests. The model of democracy which has become most widely accepted in contemporary Western political theory is undoubtedly that which Dahl calls 'polyarchal democracy'. This is an 'open' society characterized by the existence of many groups and organizations sufficiently independent, active and influential to articulate and press their demands. It contains also the legal and institutional arrangements necessary for these groups to do so: political parties and a government which adjust or accommodate conflicting demands, producing policies which sufficiently satisfy a sufficient number of interests and people to secure the necessary public and electoral support.[6] It is unnecessary to discuss this model here; we know from ordinary observation that this is certainly one way in which consent of the governed is secured. And sometimes it is a form of consent that falls at or near the upper end of our spectrum: the policies which parties or governments propose are what a considerable portion of an electorate wills, or a close enough approximation to be acceptable to a high degree. We will concentrate on other aspects of the political system which are, however, still closely related to the structure of polyarchal democracy.

One thing worth noting is that the process just described is not the only (sometimes perhaps not even the chief) way in which consent is constituted. Part of the consent upon which a government relies is rather a reflection of the approval which a large part of the community accords to the more general organization or working of the social system. The simplest, most familiar example of this point is this: We know that in times of great and widely shared economic prosperity, a considerable proportion of the electorate of democratic states votes to re-elect a government; when things go badly wrong economically there is a high probability that the government in office will be defeated, and this will usually happen whether or not the government can plausibly be said to have any responsibility for the course of events. Phases seem to occur in the history of all highly industrialized democracies which are enjoying a good rate of economic growth in which a party which is in fact fairly short on policy (a party of 'consolidation' or 'conservation') will be preferred to one eager to innovate or hasten progress; the majority is content with society much as it is, and the price of consent to a government is that things be more or less left alone. This is well known to revolutionary parties, even to many socialist parties, which have sought office within parliamentary systems.

It is an obvious point with wider application. When we examine the consent which governments secure, we should pay some attention also to the price governments must pay for the consent of the governed (or different sections of them). Analysts of democratic processes attend most to price in the form of adjustments made between competing demands. Equally important, however, may be the price that takes the form of 'immunities': understandings or assumptions made by parts of the community that certain of their interests or modes of behaviour, certain parts of the operating social system with which they are well content, will be left alone by government. These understandings are more often than not implicit or 'unconscious'; there is no explicit bargain, as in the terms of Locke's contract to maintain natural rights, that there are areas of social life into which government will not attempt to penetrate further. These 'immunities' may take innumerable forms. Businessmen would withdraw consent if aspects of economic activity were interfered with; aspects of trade unionism practice must remain inviolate for any government that hopes for the consent of that part of the governed concerned with trade unions; a government does not without great peril interfere with the free practice of religious worship. Or there may be long-standing policies which are believed to be beyond the limits of serious political discussion. Governments in Australia (even governments in which Catholics were in a majority) assumed for almost a hundred years that the standing arrangement of no state financial aid for denominational schools was an inexorable price that any government must pay to sustain a satisfactory level of consent—until Sir Robert Menzies demonstrated in a general election in 1963 that that long-established tacit understanding (with Protestants and secularists) no longer held. Since then, the question of state aid to Catholic schools has been seen to be a negotiable one within the processes of democratic electioneering.[7]

This situation we have called 'reflected consent' because it refers to the consent which a government may derive from the congruence of its own attitudes with the approval or consent for established parts of social practice which significant sections of the community manifest. Consent, in other words, is a function not only of a government's responsiveness to active pressures, demands and needs, but also of its respect for social practice to which sections of the community still strongly adhere. The same point is made in another way by Schumpeter when he argues in his *Capitalism, Socialism and Democracy* that democratic systems of government operate well only so long as governments do not attempt to extend very widely the range of their legislative concern. (Obviously, this depends on many variables. Thus Roosevelt could operate on a wider front than another president might in a period of economic growth and prosperity.)

An idea, first enunciated by Balfour in some comments on Bagehot and much employed by H. J. Laski, that has played a very prominent role in discussions of the conditions of democratic government, is the view that parliamentary democracy works only when there is throughout the community 'an agreement about fundamentals'. (Later when we speak more about consensus we shall look at this hypothesis more closely.) Agreement about fundamentals is about as indeterminate in meaning as any phrase could be, but one of its referrents might well be the kind of situation we have been describing here: namely, that in a polyarchal democracy no party could succeed in securing an acceptable level of consent, indeed the democratic constitution itself might generate a more than acceptable level of dissent, unless all parties and governments leave undisturbed certain features of the existing social organization and practice which particular minorities would struggle actively to protect. This does seem to be one characteristic of democratic systems, one usual feature of the anatomy of consent. But, of course, such a situation does not necessarily imply social agreement or consensus: it is not necessarily the *same* features of social organization that the different minorities successfully exclude from the area of permissible political consideration and negotiation.[8]

Similarly, when students of elections tell us that many electors have 'images' of the political parties, and that these images, perhaps more than concrete issues and proposals, affect their attitudes and votes,[9] this is part of what the 'image' of a party will usually contain: a notion of what sort of arrangements and modes of behaviour a party will respect and, if necessary, defend. There is a more active and a more passive or negative side: the Labour party is sympathetic to workers, the Conservative party to the rich; each party is likely both to be sensitive to the more positive demands of the classes or groups it sympathizes with and also to respect its established rights, usages and institutions. Thus, we may say that both the 'permissive' and the 'supportive' consent that a democratic government may command is consent on conditions which relate as much to what governments do *not* attempt as to what they do.

So far we have said nothing about the still stronger forms of consent: the consent which can be identified not merely with the toleration of adopted policies, nor again with the granting of permission for a government to find policies of its own, but the consent which characterizes the men who share in making policies and taking decisions where the policies and decisions may be said to give effect, in some degree, to their own will. It is well enough known that the practice of modern democracies does not base government with the consent of the governed to any great degree on this form of consent (at least so far as the great majority of citizens are concerned), and some contemporary critics of democracy who advocate the 'participative society' attack established society on these grounds.

Now, it may be that this form of consent does not much attract the large majority of citizens, and what we know of the level of political interest and activity of democratic communities suggests that this is so. There is clearly much truth in the sort of view that Shils has argued: that the normal condition of the majority of citizens in a liberal and 'civil' society is one of only occasional intense involvement in political concerns, and for the rest political attention is marginal, intermittent and low in intensity, and that this is a necessary condition for the effective working of a liberal and democratic system.[10] But before we comment on such wider issues, we should glance at other features of the organization of polyarchal democracies which are very relevant to the anatomy of consent.

These democracies possess a very elaborate and complex system of more or less organized groupings and associations, and, since this is so, a very intricate system of representation. The interests, demands, and beliefs of the members of these lower-level organizations are usually expressed by the leaders and office-bearers. These latter are often men of influence or power who may also be members of political parties or governments but who, in any case, act as spokesmen for the organizations to which they belong and who negotiate their interests with the similar spokesmen of other interest groups and organizations and with governments. They are part of the web of representation that operates throughout the community as much as are the representatives who are chosen in national elections.

If follows that the level of consent within the community as a whole will be related to the manner in which these associations operate, including the effectiveness of leaders in negotiating for their 'constituents', and the extent to which they do in fact truly represent them and enjoy their support. This indicates that the distribution of consent in a society is diffused and parcelled out throughout a polyarchal democracy, just as power is. One factor on which the level and distribution of consent will depend will be the relation of ordinary citizens organized within associations of various kinds with their leaders and spokesmen and on *their* relation in turn with the spokesmen of other groups or interests and with those who wield political authority at higher levels. Thus consent is diffused and mediated in many ways, as governments recognize when they rely on trade-union leaders, or leaders of confederations of industrialists and of scores of other organizations, to secure compliance with policy objectives. It is common ground now that it is a drastic over-simplification to talk about consent of the governed as if that were a direct relationship between a government on the one side and the mass electorate on the other. Consultation and negotiation between members of governments and the representatives of the multitude of groups and organizations has grown into a system of immense importance which complements the other constitutional system of representative democracy. It is not possible to deal realistically with the anatomy and mechanics of consent in a modern state without giving prominence to this extra-constitutional machinery of consultation and negotiation.[11]

The growth of this type of machinery of government may have resulted in the relative increase in the number and types of men who actually participate in decision making and policy formation and thus may well have widened the area of consent of the stronger types. The body of men who have direct contact with the processes of decision is in modern states certainly rather large. Yet it is also an implication of what has been said that, so far as the mass of the citizen body is concerned, the distribution and the quality or intensity of consent will in part depend on the effectiveness of the processes of organization and representation we have been speaking about. Some of the main reasons why these processes fail to perform at all well the functions just attributed to them are notorious and it may be worth while to list a few of them. First, there are the very large sections of modern communities which are not contained within any organizations or more or less organized movements of political significance, and which are in this sense leaderless and unrepresented. Second, and closely linked to this, there are the problems connected with the unequal power of organizations. The fact is that there are a few organizations—of industry and labour, professional associations, on some issues churches, and so on—which can wield great influence and the result is that a large part of the community will often not so much feel that it is oppressed by government or the state, but that its interests are swept aside by the really great power concentrations. And, third, the amount of general participation in most of the large organizations of modern societies is extremely low; top leaders and officials often become as remote and as unanswerable to the rank and file as high officials of the state itself. Thus, while the central organizations of a contemporary industrial society may have become extremely important centres of power and a very vital part of the mechanism by which power is distributed and balanced, it is much more questionable whether they have similarly become significant organs for popular involvement or participation.

But diffused consent may still be of some account if the rank and file can continue to 'identify' with its leaders and feel that the latter properly represent it in negotiations with governments and the representatives of other great interest groups, or in the general contribution they make to the shaping of policy and opinion. No doubt, the actual situation in contemporary industrialized democracies is an extremely complex one, and no doubt different organizations stand in different situations *vis-à-vis* their members. It is, at least, clear that there are always at work strong forces which tend to weaken or destroy accord between leaders and members. Such conditions as the size and bureaucratic structure of many modern organizations have been much studied and discussed.[12] Further, as an effect of the operation of the processes of consultation and negotiation, leaders often tend to become absorbed by the general administration and co-ordination of divergent interests at the national level, and to acquire attitudes and modes of thinking that widen the gap between them and those for whom they purport to speak. They are apt to grow more 'statesmanlike' and less 'partisan'; readier to take the 'national view' and to give weight to the 'public interest' than their followers would wish them to do.

There is a difficult issue here. The acquisition of the 'statesmanlike' virtues is usually applauded; it is said, indeed, that it is the function of the 'statesmen' from industry, labour, the churches, the professions, the universities, etc., to find accommodations between partisan interests and to move towards the achievement of a wider good. There is a great deal of merit in this proposition. On the other hand, the process can widen the gap between leaders and led, and cause many of the latter to feel that what they think, want or need, is not properly expressed. The most striking examples of this process are perhaps to be found in the history of the working-class movement. Leaders of Labour parties and trade unions who achieve a national standing and importance frequently move far away from the modes of thinking that first gave them their influence within the movement they represent. And this has helped to produce a not inconsiderable disillusion and apathy among members of working-class organizations. It is possible that a similar process affects the quality of representation of other interest groups and sections of the population.

This process may well be inevitable, and even necessary for the orderly and continuous adjustment of an enormous diversity of social interests and demands. This is not to say that it necessarily enhances the quality or intensity of consent. The tendency and its effects are sometimes most striking in the case of the major political parties. Parties have often tended to converge to such an extent, and parties that were originally parties of dissent and social change have moved so far in accommodating themselves to forces that support a *status quo*, that a time comes when issues and dissatisfactions which affect considerable minorities are ignored and unvoiced and significant opposition seems to have vanished. The constant effort to find adjustments and accommodations that will keep the society on an even keel can lead to the damping down of open dissent (or rather the weakening of the organs through which dissent can make itself heard effectively). When revulsion from 'consensus politics' becomes evident (as seems to have occurred in the United States, Britain, West Germany and other democratic Western countries in recent years), this is a symptom that the will and capacity of established organizations for independent activity has been weakened, and thus, also, the foundations of coherent and peaceful opposition and dissent.

These last points suggest a connection between the intensity and distribution of consent and the existence of effective opportunities for dissent. Most Western political theorists have assumed this to be true. They have argued that an authoritarian or totalitarian regime cannot be said to be based on the consent of the governed; a people managed or manipulated by censorship and other ways of selecting and restricting the variety of opinions and policy alternatives publicly presented is not governed with its own consent; a people without the opportunity to express opposition or dissent cannot truly be said to consent. And this is true even though a whole nation may appear to support, sometimes enthusiastically to endorse, the ruling regime and its policies.

How can this view be defended? One argument might be to identify consent solely with the strongest forms of consent: to say that unless a substantial part of the community participates in the policy- and decision-making processes, or at least has the opportunity to express openly its approval of, or permission for, policies put into effect, we do not have anything that really amounts to consent. (This is not an argument I am entitled to use because I have argued that the greater part of the consent that can be discovered in very democratic states is not of this kind.)

Or we may claim that if dissent cannot be voiced we lack evidence that a people does consent to its government and its policies. In an open or democratic society, the absence of dissent may be read as evidence of consent, but not in a state that does not in any case permit dissent to be expressed.

Or we may say, from our general experience of political behaviour, that states that will not permit open dissent cannot be founded on the consent of their subjects. From our knowledge of very complex societies we know that there are universal characteristics which inevitably generate conflicting beliefs, interests and demands. Identity of interests and unanimity of opinion are impossible to achieve. Therefore, we may conclude that the apparently nationwide and sometimes enthusiastic support that authoritarian rulers claim and enjoy must be attributable to the mechanisms of constraint and repression that they employ.

Both of these arguments carry weight. In Nazi Germany and Stalinist Russia no doubt there was a considerable body of genuine support for the regime. But, where opposition and dissent are likely to be punished, the facts are obscured because we cannot distinguish acquiescence and apparent approval secured by intimidation and fear from their nearest neighbours: acquiescence that arises from hopelessness or indifference, or from the habit of obedience (which some historians of Nazi Germany have said was important in the attitudes of many bureaucrats who continued in their posts from the Weimar regime), or from identification with the ideology, the aspiration and objectives of the leader. And so far as the second argument is concerned, it would be beyond belief that regimes which make such demands upon their people and are committed to such radical social change could achieve the miracle of near unanimous support.

Thus, the sensible man will conclude that when dissent is not publicly evident in a politically organized community one reason for its absence must be that dissent has been repressed. And it follows by definition that to the extent that opposition and disagreement are suppressed, consent is lacking. But, of course, it is also true by definition that when dissent is present in democracies, to that extent consent is absent there also. What is the difference between democracies and monolithic regimes?

The claim must be that it is probable that there will be a wider area of consent, more active or positive in quality, when dissent can express itself freely. Other things being equal, openly expressed dissent will tend to maximize consent. What supports that hypothesis? The main argument will be that the open, polyarchal society will, to a greater extent than any other, ensure that a larger number of distinct interests or claims are taken into account in the processes of governing and decision making and this presumably will raise the level of consent over a wider area. That at least is the deduction that seems to follow from the model of democratic systems as processes of interest adjustment and accommodation. A further point could be added: many men experience a heightened sense of freedom when they can participate in dissenting or opposition movements even if they never gain their objectives. The right to dissent, simply to stand out against that of which one disapproves, even when one knows that one's cause will never convert the majority, is an extremely important right and an important form of personal and social activity. Artists and men of letters do not usually expect deeply to influence politics and social policy, but to be able to express themselves nevertheless is essential to their existence. And even to be able to protest against what one is forced to accept will often make one's situation more tolerable, more consistent with one's human dignity. One is at least not a mere pawn, a mere carrier-out of commands; one plays a part in the 'conversation of mankind' and has some room in which one can act according to one's own lights.

This is a kind of participation which is important for the existence of personal freedom. And it is likely that the existence of wide opportunities for the expression of dissent, even where dissent does not possess enough power to make its views prevail, is a factor that sometimes feeds into the reserves of consent by which a political and social system is supported.

But sometimes only; for of course conflict and dissent cannot *always* be treated as phases in the generation of consent. Where conflict concerns issues that involve intensely felt interests of competing groups; where it is linked with an urgent struggle for power to advance or protect strongly defended interests; where power is so nearly equally distributed that conflicting groups do not readily give way; when such conditions prevail, conflict and dissent can quickly erode consent, or allow dissent and opposition to spread more widely beyond the area in which it first emerged. This was often the state of French politics during the Third Republic; and the United States has shown how dissent about such issues as the Vietnam war and race relations can spread and escalate, and come to involve institutions, such as the universities, which had been outside the range of political struggle. Thus, the ways in which consent and dissent operate, and the relations between them, are affected by a multitude of social factors; and there is no simple connection between an open, polyarchal organization of a political and

4/Theories of Consensus

Within modern social theory 'consent' has been mainly a term of political philosophy, 'consensus' mainly a term in sociology. Consent has been employed, as we have seen, in theories about the justification of political authority and in defining the duty of political obedience. It has had its place, too, in theories of liberty and democracy. Consensus appears most often in the theories sociologists advance to explain social order or cohesion. As an explanatory concept it began to become familiar in sociological writings during the nineteenth century in the work of such men as Comte, de Tocqueville and Durkheim, all of whom were preoccupied with social change and disruption and interested in the factors connected with social order and disorder.

Political philosophers have not written much about consensus nor sociologists much about consent. This may be for the same reasons that explain why social philosophers have written much more about freedom than about power, and sociologists much more about power than about freedom. The concepts of consent and freedom have moral or prescriptive overtones. They are linked to the concept of rights; they lead into questions concerning the manner in which society should be organized and political authority constituted. Consensus, like 'power', is a more purely descriptive term; both purport to refer to processes or relationships which are empirical constituents of the structure of a society. The term consensus is encountered much more frequently than the term consent in the writings of contemporary social theorists, and one reason for this may be that the interest in political philosophy has declined a little while that in the 'scientific' analysis of societies and their organization has grown. In other words, contemporary social theory has been much less interested in questions of how society might or should be organized than in questions about how it is in fact organized.

But it may also be that contemporary social theorists talk more about consensus than about consent because of a recent shift in the way in which political scientists have conceived of the nature of a democratic political system. Consent, as defined by most political philosophers in the past, carried the suggestion of a more active participation of the governed in the processes of government, while consensus is more passive in its associations. The models of democracy most fashionable in the last few years have tended to play down the scope and the reality of active popular participation in democratic political processes and have emphasized more the role of leadership and of political élites. So far as relations between governed and government are concerned, acquiescence and support have seemed to be concepts more generally relevant than consent as most political philosophers have defined it. In this way, even in descriptions of the character of democratic societies, consensus has tended to replace consent as one of the key concepts describing the nature of the support on which democratic regimes rest. Whether this is so or not, ever since the work of the nineteenth-century pioneers of contemporary sociology, a large number of sociologists have been more concerned with problems of social order and cohesion than with problems of liberty. This does not necessarily reflect an ideological bias. Many sociologists would assert that the ultimate question with which their subject is concerned as a discipline is: 'How is society possible?'

However, the two concepts are obviously closely allied. And the manner in which consent has so far been dealt with in this study —by including under consent the whole range of attitudes and relationships set out in the continuum in Chapter 2, and by the attempt to indicate the forms in which consent may manifest itself in actual societies—has brought the notion of consent very close to that of consensus. It is probable that most political philosophers would demur from this very wide conception of consent. The reader will have noticed how in an earlier chapter we silently transformed Key's phrases 'permissive consensus' and 'supportive consensus' into 'permissive' and 'supportive' *consent*; still earlier, we had pointed out that Hooker's 'silent allowances' and Locke's 'tacit consent' resemble closely the 'consensus' of the modern sociologist. Although consent has had in the past the philosophical edge I have indicated, it is also true that the two concepts have a close family connection.

Are, then, the two concepts virtually synonyms? This is not the conclusion we are suggesting. It may be that consent and consensus overlap; that some of the attitudes we have described as consent are indistinguishable from some of those that would also be described as consensus—as is indicated by our borrowing Key's expressions in an examination of consent. What is called consensus may sometimes also be a relatively 'low grade' of consent. But it is not difficult, and it is also convenient, to distinguish the two concepts. The concept of consent is properly used within a political context. It refers to possible relationships between the members of a community and those who possess political or governing authority and it refers to ways in which political authority is or may be organized and exercised. Consensus, however, has a wider, more general, range of reference. It does not refer only to relationships between governed and government, although the relationships it does refer to may be important in determining, even constituting, political relationships (as the current phrase, 'consensus politics', may suggest). Consensus refers to types of relationships which may obtain between members of a society with respect to almost all their social activities and interactions. Generally, when sociologists assert the existence of social consensus within a particular society (or assert that all stable societies are characterized by social consensus), they intend to assert the reality of relationships that enter into the constitution of the social system in its totality. We might, for example, say that if it is true of a particular society that its government enjoys the consent of the governed, the consenting of the governed would form part, but only part, of the social consensus characteristic of the society.

Consensus is a concept even more controversial and problematic than consent. There are the same types of difficulties in defining, identifying or locating it, and, as with consent, great difficulties in specifying and producing the evidence that demonstrates its existence. The sociologists who deny that modern complex societies ever do, in fact, exhibit consensus, or who at least deny that consensus is an important factor in accounting for the cohesion or stability of societies, sometimes defend their position by saying that empirical data do not suggest that social consensus does in fact exist. The data, they assert, lend themselves to a different interpretation.

It is easy to understand why there should be these differences of interpretation. Usually the asserted consensus is not a matter of direct or immediate observation. Sociologists try to characterize and account for social attitudes, behaviour and relationships, and frequently the notion of consensus is introduced as an explanation of what the situation is. Thus, the political scientist, V. O. Key, is able to say: 'The magic word "consensus", in short, solves many puzzles, but only infrequently is the term given any precise meaning.' And he says later in the same book, 'In the main the notion of consensus has sprung from the inventive minds of theorists untainted by acquaintance with mass attitudes. Knowledge of the relevant mass attitudes is slight, but such as it is, it does not give much comfort to those who suppose that most people carry around in their heads the elements of democratic theory even in the most attenuated form.'[1] However, despite his scepticism Key himself from time to time concedes that some aspects of American politics suggest the existence of a consensus of some kind, although it is another matter to say what form the consensus takes.

We shall spend some time discussing the meaning of 'consensus' before turning to some theories in which the concept is employed. It is sometimes said that the term, as a technical term of sociological theory, derives from Comte. Of course, the idea of social consensus goes back well beyond Comte; we have earlier suggested that it has a history almost as long as the history of systematic political and social speculation and that we can detect it in the political writings of Cicero or in Hooker's 'silent allowances'. It has been present wherever notions of a contractual basis of social order have been present and it has often merged into the idea of consent.

In Comte himself (and in other nineteenth-century social writers) it appears to have meanings sometimes not identical with those it has in contemporary sociology. In the *Cours de Philosophie Positive*, Comte refers to the 'radical consensus proper to the social organism' in a chapter in which he is discussing what he calls 'the fullest mutual relation between all parts of an organism', which, according to him, is the governing principle of social science. In this passage, 'consensus' appears to refer to the condition of integration or congruence of all parts of a social system: the inspiration for the use of the concept appears to be the functional interdependence of the parts of an organism. But he speaks also of the 'regular and constant convergence of an innumerable multitude of human beings, each possessing a distinct and, in a certain degree, independent existence, and yet disposed . . . to concur in many ways in the same general development'. In another place he asserts that 'authority is derived from concurrence, and not concurrence from authority'.[2] Thus for Comte the concept appears to have a wide connotation, referring to a general state of congruence, co-hesion and interdependence between the parts of a social system (or 'organism'); and 'concurrence', the identity of beliefs, attitudes, etc., that may be characteristic of the members of a society, seems to be one manifestation or mode of the more general state of 'consensus'.

J. S. Mill appears to follow the first of the meanings here attrib-uted to Comte. In Book VI of his *System of Logic*, he says that the term derives from physiology, and, referring to Comte, he says that 'consensus' relates to the fact that 'nothing that takes place in the operations of society is without its share of influence on every other part' (Ch. IX). Later, he defines consensus as 'the uniformi-ties of coexistence between the different states of the various social phenomena'. Thus for some at least of the nineteenth-century pioneers of scientific sociology who are said to have introduced the term into sociological theory, the notion of consensus is not limited in its reference to agreement about beliefs, attitudes, values, norms, objectives, etc., but is used much more widely to refer to the interdependence or inter-connectedness of the parts of a society—to what we might rather think of as the systemic character of societies.

But in more recent sociological theory the term, imprecise as it may be, is given a more restricted meaning. I. L. Horowitz pro-fesses to detect six different senses of the term in the writings of recent 'consensus theorists'.[3] These include 'adjustment of social dissension'; 'accord between role behaviour and role expectation'; shared beliefs which cut across group boundaries; a shared view concerning identity or congruence of interests. These meanings are varied and vague enough, but at least all of them seem to carry a reference to the beliefs or attitudes of members of a society *vis-à-vis* each other.

We may say, then, that in recent sociological theory the notion of consensus has not been given a meaning which makes it co-extensive with such other ideas as those of the stability, cohesion or integration of a society, or of the functional interdependence of social institutions and processes. But as it is used by most soci-ological theorists it is related to these other concepts; it is usually employed in theories which profess to explain such broad or general characteristics of societies. Some sociologists maintain that consensus of certain sorts is a necessary condition of the stability of complex and differentiated social systems. Others may connect it instead with more particular aspects or sectors of the social system; some argue, for example, that the stability of *democratic* political systems requires the existence of certain forms of consensus.

Now it seems obvious that when we say of any society that it is well-integrated or highly cohesive, or that it exhibits a high degree of stability, we have in mind a rather large number of distinguishable characteristics or relationships that either constitute, or directly contribute to, the state of the social system to which we are referring. These would include such features as the following: the absence of serious and continuing dissension; the presence of a relatively high degree of congruence between role behaviour and role expectation; the stable persistence of patterns of interaction and co-operation between individuals and groups within the economy and within the wider social framework; a relatively high measure of compliance by most members of the community with the social norms and rules which help to preserve stable patterns of interaction. And we would probably admit, as a matter of ordinary observation, that these characteristics may be supported by a number of different mechanisms.

Thus, a society may possess a high degree of cohesiveness because its members conform to norms or patterns of interaction largely as a result of unreflecting habit or custom; there are societies in which the power of custom and tradition is relatively strong. Many members of a society may regularly conform to established patterns because they are unaware of the existence of possible alternatives; or because they fear that they will be less well off if they deviate; or because they feel themselves to lack the capacity to modify established institutions and modes of behaviour; or because of overt compulsion and constraint such as the pressure of the law and its sanctions. All such processes work together to produce a measure of cohesion and stability. And it is clear that no one would wish to say that all of them are instances of what is called 'consensus'.

If we say, then, that consensus refers to characteristics of a society (or of its members) that are causally connected with the existence of social stability and cohesion, two broad problems arise. First, to specify what consensus is and what are the criteria for its existence and non-existence; and, second, to specify what kind of consensus (consensus with regard to what?) is claimed to be a necessary condition for the state of stability or cohesion. So far as the problem of defining the meaning of consensus is concerned, one difficulty is in distinguishing its meaning precisely so that it is not confused with other concepts or processes connected with social stability and integration. It is very easy to fall into a circular argument in such analyses: to take the existence of stability as the criterion of consensus and to argue that consensus is the condition that produces stability. The scepticism of political scientists such as V. O. Key concerning the use of consensus as an explanatory concept is encouraged by the frequency with which tautological assertions and circular arguments appear in discussions of this subject.

There is also another problem similar to that discovered when we were analysing consent. There is a continuum of attitudes and relationships that overlap or flow into one another and one may have trouble in deciding what is to count as consensus and what falls without the definition. If all members of a society follow uniform modes of behaviour in certain respects because they all conform in a non-reflecting way to long-established customs, is this to count as consensus? Or if one is told by a sociologist that a stable social order requires a large measure of 'value consensus' (and cannot be maintained by the continuous exercise of force) is 'value consensus' to be taken to mean that there must be conscious or deliberate acceptance of the common value system? Unless questions of this kind are faced, one cannot be sure what is being asserted by exponents of 'consensus models' who attribute to consensus a very important role in the explication of social stability and cohesion.

In his *Modern Social Theory*,[4] P. S. Cohen arrives at a definition of consensus through a discussion of conformity and compliance. In particular instances these latter may be induced by coercion, but Cohen argues that within any stable society there must always be 'some consensus on norms'. It seems that consensus on norms, in contrast with enforced compliance with them, involves *commitment*, and especially commitment to values which support the social norms. 'What is usually meant by consensus,' Cohen says, '. . . implies that adherence to norms is not based purely on inducement or coercion, but also on acceptance of certain values and on the psychological need to conform which is itself a fundamental value.' (pp. 143-4) Of course, to link consensus exclusively with conformity or compliance, or to restrict it to acceptance of common values, is to use the concept much more narrowly than it is now familiarly used in political and sociological writing; political scientists, for instance, talk about consensus in the support of political policies and objectives of policy. However, what interests us at the moment is the linking of consensus with commitment, although there is also some justification for especially emphasizing consensus in relation to norms and values. The justification is that ever since the time of Comte, consensus has been used especially in connection with the theory of social integration, and integration has been taken to be, to a considerable extent, a matter of social norms and social values.

To return to consensus and commitment. It does seem that by recent sociologists and political scientists consensus has been used to refer to two main characteristics of social structure. The first is the sense of *agreement*: the thesis that there is a harmony of a special kind that may characterize a society and its members. Secondly, by most of those who have employed it, it has been used to indicate the supposedly *voluntaristic* ingredients of social organization and integration. The concept suggests the conscious, willing or deliberate acceptance of various elements within the social system and thus it excludes, for example, conformity or 'orderliness' brought about by constraint or fear. Of course, as so defined, the concept is not easy to distinguish sharply; once again we are dealing with bands on a continuum. At one end we might have a very deliberate or considered acceptance by a large part of the population of certain common values—for example the value of democratic equality, or toleration of different religious faiths. No one would hesitate to call this an instance of consensus. But further down the continuum we come upon more equivocal cases. Is there no consensus on values unless those who participate in the consensus deliberately or reflectively embrace the values in question? If we say 'yes' to this, we rule out much that many modern 'consensus theorists' would wish to count as consensus. Thus, sociologists such as Talcott Parsons build heavily on the doctrine that social order is connected with common acceptance of systems of fundamental values, yet they also attach much weight to the processes of 'socialization' and the 'internalization' of values, processes which commence very early in life. To the extent that values and norms are 'internalized' they are likely *not* to be deliberately or reflectively adopted, though, if the process has been successful, they may be said to be freely accepted by the adult without any feeling that they have been imposed. We have already mentioned another equivocal situation: that of traditional, habitual or customary social behaviour.

Let us elaborate this latter situation. We would hesitate to say that *all* social behaviour which conforms with customary or traditional modes of behaviour can be counted as consensus. For example, if a society has a class of slaves who unthinkingly and unquestioningly perform customary roles (and not at all because of intimidation and imposed constraints), are we to say that in that society the institution of slavery is supported by a consensus? To say so would be to make consensus so inclusive a term that it would lose much of its analytical value. On the other hand, it seems that we would be imposing criteria too stringent for use if we excluded all forms of traditional and customary action. There are many cases where people experience traditions or customs as being irksome and imposing constraints they would like to throw off if only they knew how. But there are other cases, very important for the analysis of social order and cohesion, where people have come to feel that their traditions and customs have an inherent claim on their respect and obedience. Often they identify with their customs and traditions; their possession of these things often comes to characterize them as the particular social group they are; and they may even come to regard as subversive or treasonable those who oppose or flout the peculiar customs and traditions of the society. They have, in sociological jargon, 'internalized' the traditional modes of behaviour even though they rarely have occasion to become conscious of the fact. Conscious or not, there can be no doubt about their emotional attachment to customary or traditional ways, and it would be absurd not to allow that a situation of this sort counts as consensus.

We are suggesting, therefore, that what we call consensus involves either an intellectual or an emotional relation to the object which may be justly characterized as *agreement* with it. Commitment may be too strong a term for most cases; consensus may not generally or usually be a matter of consciousness, and still less of explicit belief, but at least it suggests some degree of positive attachment or adherence to whatever may be the object of the consensus. Once again, we are dealing with attitudes, either cognitive or emotional, and we are arguing that the state of consensus involves what may be called 'agreement' of a two-dimensional kind: the agreement of the members of a social group with one another with regard to their attitude or relation to certain objects, and agreement also in the sense of their attachment or adherence to those objects. Conforming behaviour which is similar in its external manifestations may be the expression of very different attitudes, and it is the latter which are significant for determining whether there is consensus or not. And, of course, attitudes, all of which may be characterized as attitudes of agreement with or adherence to, may vary greatly in degree of intensity. It is not important to draw sharp lines between what counts as consensus and what does not in cases that fall near the margin; what is important is that we should agree that consensus contains at its core a positive agreement with or adherence to whatever the consensus is said to be 'about'.

Consensus, therefore, is not merely uniformity of behaviour or conformity by all or most of the members of a group to certain patterns of action. It is uniformity and conformity that are connected with a certain class of attitudes. We have taken for granted another point, that consensus has to be defined in relation to particular *objects*—persons, beliefs, values, institutions or whatever. Thus, there are other types of solidarity or unity that may be extremely important for the cohesion of social groups which would have to be distinguished from consensus because the solidarity is not forged around common objects. For instance, the intense bonds of affection and mutual loyalty that may be present among the members of a family or kinship group, or the 'consciousness of kind' that some social theorists have spoken about in connection with social or national solidarities, are not, as far as they go, examples of consensus although they may form the basis for the development of consensus or may be strengthened by its existence. Indeed, complex societies usually find means of strengthening some of these more immediate ties by deliberately developing symbolical and other objects of common attachment.

These elementary points may seem so obvious as to be not worth stating. Yet sociologists, who have preferred to give most of their attention to arguing about the much more complicated and obdurate problems of the role of consensus in supporting stability and cohesion, have usually been rather casual in specifying a core of meaning for the concept of consensus. In consequence the significance of the claims they make in relation to the large question is often obscure. Defining the term 'consensus' is not important in itself; it is important only because of the invocation of the term in wider theories about social integration and stability.

Some contemporary sociologists distinguish between 'consensus theorists' and 'conflict theorists'. Roughly the distinction is between those who attribute a large role in the maintenance of the stability of social systems to consensus and those who emphasize the ubiquity and fundamental role of conflict of various sorts, and who think of societies as being rather balances of conflicting forces, the balance being preserved usually by the exercise of power. Thus, Durkheim might be classified as a consensus theorist. It is true that Durkheim was critical of the role that Comte attributed to moral consensus in social integration, and was himself interested in the complicated mechanisms and conditions of integration which are present in, and necessary for, any society characterized by an advanced state of division of labour and social differentiation; but he also maintained a strong interest in the importance of moral factors in social solidarity. In his thesis of the *conscience collective*, and his studies of the forms of religious life, he pursued his lifelong preoccupation with moral and consensual elements in social solidarity.[5]

Marx, on the other hand, is usually considered the father of 'conflict theorists'. His deterministic view of the 'forces' and 'relations' of production separated him from the voluntarism of thinkers who stressed the causal influence of a consensus of moral and social belief. His doctrine of class conflict and of class ideologies both decried the voluntaristic explanations of systems of social ideas, and also tended to deny their independent causal efficacy by making them the product and the instruments of class interests. Obviously, in Marx's model of a capitalist society, force and conflict have a more central place than they have in the models of thinkers who stress the function of consensus in social integration. These broad theoretical oppositions are still present in contemporary sociological theory.

However, these are 'models' and thus over-simplifications; the opposition between 'conflict' and 'consensus' models can be misleading. No social theorist will really deny that conflict of many different kinds is characteristic of all complex societies. Or that power, in the sense of imposed constraints, enters into the ordering of all complex social systems. On the other hand, no one could deny that there are also areas of agreement within any organized, stable society, although, in relation to any particular society, students may well disagree on the extent of the area of agreement, what the agreement embraces and the intensity of commitment by the members of the society to whatever it is the consensus is supposed to embrace. And beyond such issues, there will usually be disagreement about the more 'theoretical' question concerning the functions of consensus and conflict in maintaining or contributing to the stability and/or instability of the society. The opposition is between different views about the significance and precise roles of consensus and dissensus or conflict in relation to the stability of a social system.[6]

Thus, according to the simplified model of a complex society presented by social theorists of a more pluralistic type, society is represented as being from one point of view a system of divergent or conflicting interests and demands. These conflicting interests may be contained within a moving equilibrium or state of adjustment by the managed articulation of interests, by compromise, by bargaining and negotiation, by the emergence of balances of power. This, or something very like it, is the model of a democratic political system that has been most favoured by Western political sociologists in recent years. But those who present such a model add that the processes by which conflicting interests assert themselves and reach accommodations go on to a considerable extent within an encompassing framework of consensus.[7] Other theorists, who may be labelled 'consensus theorists', might find in society a more substantial unity or solidarity, woven out of shared beliefs, shared moral ideas and attitudes, shared social objectives. (Later we shall say more about the elements of consensus and dissensus, the different interpretations of the significance for social cohesion or stability, emphasized by different social theorists.)

These differences of perspective also affect the analysis of particular types of social relationship and process. One example is the interpretation of authority and power. We have already quoted Comte's dictum that 'authority is derived from concurrence and not concurrence from authority'. Of course, the notion of 'legitimate authority', authority based on or legitimated by acceptance of it by members of a social group, is now a sociological commonplace. But in the analysis of authority, and especially of power, while it is easy enough to make conceptual or 'analytic' distinctions, it is not at all easy in actual circumstances to say where authority deriving from common acceptance ends and where authority deriving from constraint or the fear of sanctions begins. When we are considering a large and complex social group realism compels us to admit that the two different processes are inextricably inter-twined. C. Wright Mills is a sociologist who sees power chiefly as the imposition of the interests or demands of one power-holding individual or group on others. Talcott Parsons presents power rather as a 'medium of exchange'. In effect, he emphasizes its consensual basis and treats it as an investment lodged by the members of a collectivity with the political authorities for the sake of collective purposes.[8] This is a less pluralistic view which has affiliations with and is perhaps partly derived from the tradition of philosophical political idealism with its conception of society as ideally an integrated whole and the supreme political authority the expression of the social totality. The 'common sense' view might be that power as empirical phenomenon exhibits both dimensions. Which dimension a theorist chooses to emphasize may have some-thing to do with his own temperament, values and expectations.

Let us turn from these more general points about the mean-ing of consensus to consider briefly some of the theories about the connections between consensus and social organization and sta-bility. On this level the central question is one which we have already referred to in passing: What social consensus is consensus about? Obviously, within any society there may be consensus about many different things. But what are the important types of consensus for the maintenance of social order and stability? And how does such consensus operate in supporting stability?

One type of social theory attributes a particularly central role to social norms and to common systems of values which support the norms. Stable or persistent patterns of interaction between individ-uals and groups within a society require norms which define the roles, duties, rights and claims or expectations of interrelated or interacting members of the society; a large measure of common acceptance of such norms is a condition for social integration and stability. The general acceptance of these structurally crucial norms is connected with the general acceptance of value systems which underpin the norms. According to Talcott Parsons, 'the value system of a society is, then, the set of normative judgements held by the members of a society who define, with specific refer-ence to their own society, what to them is a good society . . . With all these qualifications, it is still true to say that values held in common constitute the primary reference point for the analysis of a social system as an empirical system.'[9] In an earlier work, *The*

Structure of Social Action, Parsons, then expounding Durkheim, said, '. . . it is a fact that social existence depends to a large extent on a moral consensus of its members, and the penalty of its too radical breakdown is social extinction'. And again, '. . . it is evident that in these terms the integration of a social group consists in the common recognition on the part of its members of a single, integrated body of norms as carrying moral authority . . . A society, as Durkheim expressed it, is a moral community, and only in so far as it is such does it possess stability . . . at least to the extent neccesary to guarantee the minimum of order there must be a sharing of systems of value, there must be a system of common values.'[10] Parsons is expounding what he took to be Durkheim's view, but it is hardly to be doubted that these statements express, at least in a general way, his own conceptions of social integration. The doctrine that social integration depends upon the acceptance of a common system of values is at all events a widely held view; to quote another typical passage from another sociologist, 'No society can maintain itself if the consciences of most of its citizens are out of tune with the norms. The everyday operation of the system requires that there be a high degree of moral consensus.'[11]

Now, the statements just quoted are all very general and thus not very illuminating; they leave many questions unanswered. To begin with, it is obvious that in a complex industrial society there is always a considerable measure of moral *dissensus*, or at least deviance from accepted moral norms. For example, there are not inconsiderable minorities who deviate from (and some who positively reject) values and norms connected with sexual relations and monogamous marriage. Inspection also shows that there is a considerable measure of dissensus in relation to moral or value assumptions about political, economic and social equality and inequality, or concerning the 'justice' of existing allocations of rewards, rights and responsibilities. Again, there is dissensus regarding such matters as recognition of liberties of various kinds as against social 'order' or moral propriety. There is even dissensus in democratic industrial societies concerning the importance of such values as material welfare and growth as against other goals of human striving that may be weighted against them. It is a bold assumption by Parsons that there is necessarily a common 'value system of a society' which defines what is a 'good society'. And it is often the case that these moral, or ideological, differences are linked with the conflicting interests and demands that express themselves in political life. Moreover, in so far as we can identify predominant values and norms which appear to influence or to order the behaviour of the majority, it still remains to consider the intensity with which different members or sections of a society adhere to different components of the common value system and also the extent to which orderliness or uniformity of behaviour which may appear to manifest value consensus in fact arise from relatively unthinking or apathetic following of established patterns of behaviour. Or again, there are questions about the extent to which conformity is supported by a persisting distribution of power or influence within a society. And beyond these more particular questions there is the fundamental one concerning the significance of values as such as causal elements within a persistent and integrated structure of social behaviour—a question too complex and difficult to be dealt with in this book. These are the questions explored by so-called 'conflict theorists' in their criticisms of 'consensus theorists' such as Talcott Parsons.

We may say, however, that some of the evidence of empirical social science justifies these sceptical questions. To mention just one example, Myrdal in his famous book *An American Dilemma*,[12] makes a great deal of the ambiguities, inconsistencies and incoherences in Americans' attachment to the 'American creed'—for instance, a willingness to profess assent to it on the most abstract level, accompanied by an unwillingness to extend its application to particular classes of citizens. Other empirical studies of popular adherence to 'value systems' of the 'ultimate' or very general sort —for example, adherences to the values or principles of the democratic creed—have revealed the same assent in the abstract and rejection in concrete cases. We shall be saying more about these ambiguities in the next chapter.

On the other hand, there are counter-considerations, and it does seem plausible to assert that *some* type and measure of value consensus is a necessary condition of stability and integration. It is also a plausible hypothesis that in the course of industrial development, as Western societies have become more tightly integrated and the interdependence of individuals and social groups more continuous, direct and crucial, certain kinds of consensus about values and norms have become more important for stability. The discipline and the regularity of behaviour demanded of individuals by the requirements of advanced industrialization would scarcely be forthcoming unless the great majority shared the ultimate values and goals of the society, such goals as material welfare and steadily rising levels of monetary income and standards of living. The 'embourgeoisement' of the working class (of which Marxists used to complain) and the surrender of the masses to the values of a bureaucratic-technological consumer society denounced by contemporary political and moral rebels, represent the growth of consensus about value systems which highly integrated industrial systems both encourage and perhaps require. And these societies involve great inequalities in the distribution of rewards, roles, responsibilities and powers. Tight integration and close interdependence might be expected to generate high conflict potentials and it is not easy to imagine that such societies could preserve stability merely or chiefly by the continuous exercise of power or by the force of custom or tradition. It is reasonable to assume that a high measure of consensus, in the sense of widely shared adherence to a set of basic values and objectives, is a necessary condition of stability.

There are structurally vital institutions and forms of relationships which may be said to rest largely on the willing adherence of the greater part of the population. This is no doubt true, for example, of the family in Western societies, and also of the established rights and duties associated with the institution of property. Probably no serious social thinker believes that law and legal authority alone could preserve such institutions without the foundation of a considerable measure of moral consensus. Similarly with the broad system of social status: the status, authority and respect enjoyed by holders of certain offices, members of different professions, persons performing various types of social role, must depend on a widely accepted estimation of the respect to be accorded to them. And this allocation of deference or respect in the more diffuse and less specified ways must be a very central factor so far as social ordering and stability are concerned. All such points are no doubt common ground now with sociologists and social philosophers. Thus, we may accept the assertion that a great deal of what constitutes the fabric of belief, attitude, moral adherences or prejudices exists in the form of a consensus as we have defined it.

But even when we grant all such considerations some problems still remain. There are or have been societies in which, despite a 'high degree of moral consensus' applying to a number of areas of social relationship, conflict and instability have nevertheless been rife. At what points within a social system is consensus crucial, at what points are its presence or absence of less or little significance? When Dahrendorf says (stating the position he rejects) that 'every functioning social structure is based on a consensus of values amongst its members', and (stating the view he accepts) that 'every society is based on a coercion of some of its members by others'[13] what is he saying? In particular, what does the phrase 'is based on' mean in this connection? Is consensus or, alternatively, coercion being said to be a sufficient or a necessary condition of social stability? One would think that neither is sufficient, that both are necessary conditions of a 'functioning social structure'— at least of the structures of industrial societies. If this is granted, we may again ask: Are there any areas of social interaction, or any parts of social structure, where consensus is *especially* crucial for the maintenance of a functioning society?

Many sociologists have explicitly or implicitly addressed themselves to this question. Shils has suggested that consensus exists when there is a wide measure of agreement on the decisions to be made about the allocation of scarce values (authority, status, rights, wealth, income, etc.) and about the permissible range of disagreement; when the institutions through which decisions about such allocations are made are widely accepted; and when unequal allocations are accepted for other reasons than the expectation of coercion and enforcement. Shils takes this social area to be the main focus of consensus and dissensus and it is interesting that 'conflict theorists' usually take it as the area in which the most important conflicts of interest are engendered. There is an obvious reason for assuming this to be one of the vital regions: if it is true at all that consensus and dissensus are crucial for social stability, then this would be a locus of social organization where consensus and its absence would tell. This should be an important test case.

Now in all non-traditional, industrial societies the distribution of scarce 'values' has been the source of intense conflict and dissensus and of much political and social instability. It is not necessary to dwell on the political and industrial turbulence that has accompanied the growth of industrialization in all Western countries. On the other hand, these industrial societies, for all their periods of political and economic turbulence or instability, have also had long periods of relative stability; throughout the last two centuries they have existed as 'functioning societies' although, of course, some, such as Britain and the United States, have enjoyed greater political and social stability than others, such as France, Italy and Germany. The main point is that rather intense conflict and dissent have been able to coexist with a sufficient measure of continuity, persistence or stability in patterns of social interaction and inter-relationship throughout most of the history of most of the Western industrialized countries.

How do we explain this? What has enabled these industrial systems (and in some cases the political systems) to continue to operate with a considerable measure of continuity and stability; why have they not been disrupted more by persistent sporadic conflict or destroyed by class war? Processes of different sorts have clearly been at work, not all of them associated with consensus. Within the productive system the mutual dependence of individuals and classes on one another has obviously been a restraining force. In the relations between employers and employees inequalities of power and the availability of constraints and forms of coercion have helped to circumscribe conflict and maintain stability; with industrial workers fear of sanctions of different sorts (for example, periods of unemployment) has also been a restraining force. Those who prefer conflict models of social organization can find plenty of grist for their mills in the analysis of industrial relations, or of wider systems of social allocation or distribution.

For our purposes the relevant question is: Are there *also* forces generated by consensus which must be introduced to account for the level of stability that normally exists? How much consensus there is in a particular society, and what composes it, are empirical questions which are exceedingly hard to answer. And, before we could answer them, another general point connected with the phrase we have just used—'the level of stability'—must be borne in mind. Stability is itself a matter of more or less; all highly developed and highly differentiated societies manifest at all times a great deal of instability of many different kinds. As regards any concrete social system we can ask what aspects of the social system have been more stable than others, and how much stability each different aspect has in fact manifested. We can ask whether, for society as a whole, stability at some points or in some areas is more crucial than at others. We can distinguish with regard to a partic-ular society different degrees of stability, and also, so to speak, different layers of stability.

Let us return, for example, to the area of industrial relations. In most capitalist societies we can speak about stability at some levels and instability at others. Thus, in most industrialized Western countries, the great majority of the working class has rejected in practice the Marxian image of itself as a revolutionary class, dedicated to the overthrow of capitalism. Similarly it has rejected the Sorellian 'myth' of the general strike: the general strike has occurred seldom if at all in the history of modern industrial countries. Thus in the broad structure of 'class' relationships within the capitalist industrial system there has been a great deal of stability (which has not been incompatible with significant change). At a lower level, the industrial strike concerned with a particular industrial issue has been a very common phenomenon, although such strikes have not occurred so frequently or on such a scale as to disrupt the stability, continuity or growth of the industrial system in most Western countries.

The point is, then, that if we are talking about stability (and about the role consensus plays in supporting it) it may well be true that different forms of consensus will be important in different areas of social organization, at different levels of social stability.

We may be thinking of social stability in the sense of the non-occurrence of political revolution, in which case we are thinking mainly about what Shils calls 'the centre' in contrast with 'the periphery'—that is, the central institutions of political authority and administration, and also what he calls 'the central value system', the values and norms that define and support the structures of central authority.[14] And if we ask why revolutionary trends or potentials of Western proletariats have not developed further, it seems very likely that widely shared adherences to central value systems and institutions (and not merely coercion or habituation), are important factors. We may be able to distinguish a number of strands in such a consensus. One might be the sense of membership in a community, a sense of identity with it, and an aversion from anything that threatens to disrupt it by large-scale civil disorder. The central political institutions may have a considerable measure of 'legitimacy'. There may be a widespread sentiment in favour of law-abidingness.

These are examples of attitudes towards the central system of authority. But these central institutions may also be supported by other forms of consensus. It may be true, for instance, that the majority in all sections of industrial societies have so far adhered with some intensity to the values of 'material welfare', the continuous pursuit of economic growth, steadily rising standards of living for all. It is possible that such values have been dominant throughout a very wide section of industrial communities, perhaps at the expense of other possible common values such as the further development of values inherent in a democratic ideology. Such a consensus about the 'material' values of an industrial society could, of course, become explosive—a powerful 'negative consensus'—if the political and economic systems proved incapable of meeting expectations. It is plausible, however, to assume that so far in the history of the Western industrial countries, or of most of them, such a consensus has provided these societies with broad, common objectives and has strengthened the consensual support for the central political institutions and the values and norms associated with them.

This is connected with a particular view of the role of consensus. This view is that consensus contributes to political and social stability because the beliefs, attitudes and objectives which a large part of the community holds in common operate to limit and circumscribe the conflicts that do arise. We have already referred to a passage by R. A. Dahl which expresses this idea.* It may be said that the members of a society, for the sake of maintaining or pursuing ways of living and objectives they all share, refrain from pursuing their conflicts to the point at which these common interests would be endangered. This provides a powerful motive for finding accommodations when conflict does appear. There can be no doubt that such binding forces do function in complex stable societies although they may often be latent or implicit—for instance, a widely spread support for law and order may manifest itself only when some group attacks law and order. And there are no doubt strongly dissident groups in most societies which are restrained from attacking existing arrangements because of the sensed weight of the consensus that supports them. This is recognized by critics of existing 'technological society' who attack consensual politics as one of the forces of oppression.

According to this conception of its role, consensus not only provides a force that encourages the finding of accommodations between conflicting interests and demands, it also limits the area and the issues of conflict. There are a number of different mechanisms at work here also. There is consensus on policy objectives of the sort that the disagreements that do arise in political life are simply matters of adjusting conflicting opinions or demands within

* See note 7.

the framework of a wider agreement. Again, in the large democratic states there is always the need to select the issues of political
debate and decision at any given time; it is probable that the
stability, coherence and effectiveness of the political system depend
on the efficiency of the process of selection. When the political
system is overloaded with too many disparate issues, when a large
number of the community's established social arrangements are
unsettled and become the subject of active political controversy,
the system will be unstable. But when there is high stability, there
is enough consensus to prevent the greater part of the social nexus
from being made the subject of political activity. Such consensus
may concern basic foundations of policy about which there is such
wide agreement that no issue arises, as in the case of widely accepted principles of a nation's foreign policy or a policy of pro-
tective tariffs. Or the consensus may concern matters about which
in fact there is great disagreement throughout the community, but
also an agreement that such matters are not to be made the subject
of political debate—as with the agreement to 'keep religion out of
politics'. Generally speaking, stable political systems (where the
stability cannot be attributed mainly to coercion) rest to a quite
considerable extent on forms of consensus which protect very
large sectors of the established system of social relationships from
becoming spheres of political attention and activity.

Thus contemporary sociologists and political scientists for the
most part attribute the stability of political societies (especially
democratic polities) to a balance between consensus and dissensus.
Talcott Parsons, discussing the implications of American electoral
studies, speaks of democratic elections as contributing to the 'maintenance of a moving balance between general agreement on some
values and well distributed disagreement on others', the social
condition which he calls 'the limited polarization of the society'.[15]
However, although this has become more or less common ground,
there is considerable disagreement about the interconnections of
consensus and dissensus. Thus, many sociologists support the
view that *one* of the factors which enable societies characterized by
a considerable range and intensity of conflict to remain stable is
that there is a consensus in support of the established procedures
and processes whereby conflicting interests and demands are expressed and decisions made. This theory is extended to include the
political institutions. But if we further ask what are the conditions
for the existence of the consensus that supports the decision

making or governing institutions, disagreement emerges. Some maintain that this consensus depends in turn on a basic consensus concerning social value systems, social institutions, certain central social goals or objectives. The doctrine that Western-style democratic political institutions have rested upon a deeper social agreement about 'fundamentals' has enjoyed a long life in the theory of democracy. But others strongly reject this notion that 'agreement about fundamentals' has been a necessary condition of the consensual (or widely shared support for) democratic forms and processes of government. This controversy has been so prominent in the theory of democracy that we shall reserve a discussion of it until the following chapter.

We may, however, at this point glance at the view of those who think that agreement about the 'rules of the game' is the one and *only* form of consensus needed to account for political stability in democratic societies. C. J. Friedrich is one who rejects the assumption that the stability of democratic parliamentary systems of government requires 'agreement about fundamentals'. He argues that 'the issue of legitimacy shows that there ought indeed to be a *measure* of agreement on one fundamental, and that is the kind of rule that is right and the sort of ruler who is entitled to rule. In a democracy this question will be settled in a constitution (written or unwritten), and an acceptance of the "rules of the game" laid down in the constitution will be the one basic agreement required.'[16] Similarly Eckstein attributes the unusually large measure of stability which the British system of government has long exhibited not to a wide area of agreement about basic values or objectives or policies, but to the strength of the adherence of the British people to their political institutions. 'In essence, the British invest with a very high affect the procedural aspects of their government and with low affect its substantive aspects; they behave like ideologists in regard to rules and like pragmatists in regard to policies.'[17] And again E. Haas: '. . . we may think of modern nation states as communities whose basic consensus is restricted to agreement on the procedures for maintaining order and settling disputes among groups, for carrying out well understood functions. Unlike that of the Functionalist, this conception pre-supposes agreement merely on the means of achieving welfare, but not on the context of laws and policies, not on the substance of the functions.'[18]

But this does not appear to be a very plausible view. It is true that in many societies widespread and powerful sentiments have grown in support of some parts of the institutions and procedures of government—the monarch, the constitution and so on. It is probably true that the capacity of political procedures—'rules of the game'—to preserve their sway requires that some small minority of the society, some combination of 'élites', both understand what they are and are vigilant and meticulous in upholding them. But the evidence of electoral studies and surveys of popular political attitudes does not suggest that most citizens of modern industrial societies have either a clear understanding of, or intense or consistent attachment to, the values and principles of democratic political procedures. (This is a point we shall deal with more fully in the next chapter.) Much evidence suggests that, despite the increased integration of large-scale industrial states, and the ever-growing extent to which governments interact with the activities of individuals and groups, a large part of the public feels itself to be remote from and comparatively indifferent about the forms of the *central* institutions of government and their values. Admittedly it is not easy to interpret such evidence with confidence, but at least it forces us to be wary about the manner in which we speak about 'agreement about the centre' or consensus about the 'central value system' (to quote from Shils). It also makes us cautious about claiming that consensual support for the central institutions of authority is either the sole or the chief form of consensus necessary for the stability of a democratic state.

Of course, if we were seriously to attempt to analyse the forces and relationships supportive of a central political system, we would need to deal with a number of different things. We might concede that, since normally the majority in a democratic society does continue to accept, and to participate in the operation of, the democratic procedures—elections and so on—there is 'supportive consensus', to use Key's term. But this would not take us far. As we shall argue in the next chapter, the consensus of beliefs, attitudes, sentiments, etc., which provides this support is itself far from being a coherent, cohesive and stable structure. The attitudes of those who may be said to share in the consensus ('the public' of the consensus as Shils expresses it) differ widely in intensity. And also the structure of beliefs and attitudes of the consensus is usually flawed by ambiguities and ambivalences; it has no great measure of consistency or coherence. In addition it could be argued that this consensual structure needs to be underpinned by other types of consensus and that it is likely to crumble if these are removed.

One supporting area of consensus would be the accommodations between conflicting interests and demands that have been reached over a period of time, and which the groups concerned are willing to accept for the time being as a base from which further demands can be projected. These accommodations become the substance of a social consensus which protects the political institutions from excessive pressure. This is the point made when we considered how consensus about economic and social questions limits and helps to select the issues which become active on the political level. It has been well put by V. O. Key: 'Doubtless, too, the cumulation of individual issues on which supportive consensus prevails contributes to the stability of the political order as a whole. As policy after policy comes to be underpinned by such support, the adaptation of a wider and wider range of government activity to new necessities becomes a matter of detail rather than the occasion for the renewal of deepseated controversy on basic issues.'[19]

In a stable democracy issues get settled and the settlement becomes part of the structure of the society, at least for a time. Thus the processes of accommodation inherent in democratic party politics extend and strengthen areas of consensus concerned with economic and social arrangements. It is true that this process has been more clearly manifest in some countries than in others; more, for example, in Britain than in France, where issues disruptive of political stability (including some concerned with the basic constitution of the state) have stayed alive though dormant for periods from the Revolution to the outbreak of the Second World War and beyond. Moreover, with modern democratic states, generally acceptable accommodations are not only arrived at *through* the procedures or institutions of the state. The state has itself become an agency which directly provides and administers social services and these activities are built into the very structure of the state (as the expression 'welfare state' suggests): this, then, is another reason for the widely shared acceptance of established political procedures and institutions. When Eckstein says of the British that they behave like ideologists in regard to rules and like pragmatists in regard to policies, this is undoubtedly to exaggerate the intensity, purity and extent of attachment to rules and procedures (or, more widely, institutions of government) for their own sakes.

Without doubt a quite general agreement about rules and procedures is a necessary condition of political stability; by definition
a society is not stable if there exists intense conflict concerning the
very structure of its central institutions of authority. But it is very
difficult to conceive that acceptance of the constitutional rules of
the game is 'the one basic agreement required', that 'basic consensus'
could be restricted to 'agreement on the procedures for maintaining order and settling disputes'. It is difficult to conceive that there
could be this sort of agreement in a relatively free and democratic
society unless there existed also other widely extended areas of
consensus which served to contain and moderate the pressures
which might otherwise discharge themselves against the political
system itself. It would scarcely be plausible to assert that agreement about 'the rules of the game' can coexist with any sort and
volume of economic and social conflict.

We must now consider the doctrine, which has quite a long
history, that the procedures or institutions of democracy can operate peacefully and effectively only within those communities in
which there is a deep-seated agreement about 'fundamentals'—
where 'fundamentals' is *not* taken to mean the constitutional
arrangements of the society.

5 / Consensus and Democracy

In this chapter we shall carry further the discussion of the kinds of consensus (if any) that support the stability of democratic processes or institutions. We have suggested reasons for doubting that the one type of consensus necessary is agreement to support 'rules of the democratic game'. We also briefly suggested some reasons for doubting that a stable democratic system requires a wide consensus in support of the 'values' of democracy; we inclined to the conclusion of H. J. McClosky that '. . . contrary to the familiar claim, a democratic society can survive despite widespread popular misunderstanding of and disagreement about basic democratic and constitutional values'.[1] (We shall say more about this question of consensus about democratic values.) We have indicated other sorts of consensus that would seem of some importance for the stable operation of a democratic polity and this aspect of the problem we intend here to explore further. We shall begin by commenting especially on a formulation that many political theorists have thought to be satisfactory: that democratic institutions have proved to be stable and secure in some societies because matters about which citizens disagree are much less 'fundamental' than those about which they agree. This view has most frequently been advanced by English writers as an explanation of the stability of British democracy, but it has sometimes been generalized in the form that agreement about fundamentals is a necessary condition for the stable and peaceful (or efficient) working of a democracy of the Western type.

But first it is worth emphasizing why the stability of democratic systems may be thought to pose a very special problem. Liberal democratic systems include the following norms and characteristics. The rule of law (which prescribes that governments, and all those exercising the authority of the state, must themselves conform to rules of law clearly prescribed); the open, legal competition for office and power by rivals; the choice of governments by popular election and the acceptance of the 'verdict' of the electorate;

respect by those in power for the rights of organized, open opposition, including opposition parties seeking to displace those in office; equally, the willingness of those defeated in elections to comply with the decisions of a constitutionally chosen government, not resorting to force, violence or other undemocratic methods to resist its authority. And doubtless one could extend this list.

The special problem of democracies is this: these norms or characteristics appear to demand so great a degree of tolerance and self-restraint on the part both of those in power and out of power that it is not unnatural to assume that there must be some force that produces such tolerance and restraint. By definition, conformity to a democratic constitution is not secured by coercion; the tolerances and restraints are voluntarily maintained. Yet at the same time, the conditions of vast, highly industrialized and differentiated societies in which wealth, power and opportunities are so unequally distributed would seem to generate the potentialities of conflict of the most disruptive kind. Democracies, while they retain their democratic characteristics, do not suffer such disruption. Why should this be?

J. S. Mill in his essay on Coleridge discusses the 'conditions of permanent political society'. The second of the conditions he distinguishes he calls 'the feeling of allegiance or loyalty' which may attach itself to different social objects. But 'whether in a democracy or in a monarchy, its essence is always the same; viz., that there be in the constitution of the State *something* which is settled, something permanent, and not to be called in question.' And Mill proceeds to maintain that

> A State never is, nor, until mankind are vastly improved, can hope to be, for any long time exempt from internal dissension; for there neither is, nor has ever been, any state of society in which collisions did not occur between immediate interests and passions of powerful sections of the people. What, then, enables society to weather these storms, and pass through turbulent times without any permanent weakening of the securities for peaceable existence? Precisely this—that however important the interests about which men fall out, the conflict did not affect the fundamental principles of the system of social union that happened to

exist; nor threaten large portions of the community with the subversion of that on which they had built their calculations, and with which their hopes and aims had become identified.[2]

Mill is not very explicit about the 'fundamental principles of the social system' that remain unquestioned. No doubt he includes fundamental constitutional principles, but his reference to those things on which many had set their hopes suggests he would include other things as well. Of course, there is an ambiguity in this that is relevant to the exploration of consensus; the fact that interests which powerful sections of the community consider vital are not threatened by political action does not necessarily imply that there is general agreement in support of those interests. We have made this distinction before and will return to it again. Another well-known expression of a view similar to Mill's is Lord Balfour's dictum: 'Our whole political machinery presupposes a people so fundamentally at one that they can safely afford to bicker.'[3] Or, as Friedrich states Balfour's doctrine for him: '. . . democracy based on the ability to agree to disagree is possible only when there are no disagreements serious enough to be dubbed fundamental'.

The hypothesis then is that within a stable democracy there is so to speak a substratum of unity or agreement so powerful that it can counteract the divisive and disruptive forces arising from conflicting beliefs and interests. That about which the members of the community are united is more 'fundamental' than those things about which they disagree and conflict. Does this substratum account for the cohesion of political democracies?

Friedrich attacks this hypothesis. In effect, he argues that 'agreement upon fundamentals' is a condition or requirement of totalitarian systems, not of democracies; that it is in fact a distinguishing trait of democracies that they are hospitable to a wide diversity of disagreement about 'fundamental' matters—beliefs, ways of life, interests, demands. But this argument seems to miss the point of the doctrine for two reasons. First, if there exists within a community a widespread agreement on matters considered to be fundamental, and if that agreement is spontaneous—that is, not engineered by coercion, suppression and the like—this is not necessarily an undemocratic state of affairs; and, second, depending on how one defines 'fundamental', a considerable measure of diversity and conflict is compatible with the existence of a considerable measure of agreement about other things. In most liberal societies there exists a wide diversity of religious creeds, and many of those who profess them consider them to be vital or fundamental. If there also exists a widely and strongly felt agreement on the principle of tolerating diverse religious professions, then this is an example of consensus about something 'fundamental' which is compatible with disagreement about other things also considered to be 'fundamental'. And it may well be the case that in countries which do contain large groups of differing religions, or different linguistic groups, that agreement about this fundamental of toleration is a necessary condition for the survival of democratic political processes.

There is another difficulty about the idea that democratic systems require, or work best when there is, an agreement about fundamentals. It is the difficulty of saying what *is* fundamental—except in a tautologous way. It is unilluminating to assert that those principles or interests are fundamental which some powerful group will use force, if necessary, to protect. If we say that the fundamentals which must remain unquestioned are the basic rules or procedures of a democratic polity, we are saying nothing more sensational than that democratic processes will not work peacefully and effectively if there are powerful sections of the community that oppose and attack them. What, then, are the fundamentals that must be generally accepted if a democratic system is to preserve its stability?

Some political theorists, influenced by Marxist doctrine, have identified property interests and relations (within capitalist society) as the substructure of the fundamental interests that have to be respected. H. J. Laski used to maintain that a socialist party coming to office in a democratic way would be unable to effect a peaceful democratic transition to socialism because capitalists consider their property interests so fundamental they would resort to force and any other anti-democratic methods to maintain them. Thus, he concluded in line with Marx's and Lenin's conceptions of the nature of capitalist society and capitalist democracy, that within a capitalist society democratic institutions could work only provided the broad structure of the capitalist economy was accepted as a 'fundamental' that must not be attacked by legislation.

But this example shows the difficulty of pointing to social interests or aspects of social organization as being especially fundamental;

it is doubtful whether the history of many of the 'capitalist democracies' during the last twenty or thirty years has confirmed Laski's judgement. In most of these countries legislation has modified rather profoundly the character and rights of property, and the structure and control of the economic system. As Schumpeter argued in some detail in *Capitalism, Socialism and Democracy*, capitalists have not merely had forced upon them, but in some cases have voluntarily accepted, steadily expanding governmental direction and regulation. In some countries they have not seriously resisted the nationalization of industries which occupy a key position in the whole economy; in all countries in varying degrees they have acquiesced in new measures for the greater governmental management of the total economy. The main social developments, both international and national, which have contributed to the peaceful acceptance of this restructuring of economic systems and this transformation of the pattern of economic direction and control are generally familiar. Now, it can hardly be said that the policies which have brought about these changes have been concerned with relatively minor or non-fundamental aspects of the social system; with matters so relatively unimportant that politicians and political parties could safely be allowed 'to bicker' about them. It is clear that even interests which powerful groups may consider to be vital can change; individuals and groups may come to define their interests differently and to see differently how their interests can be protected, or advanced; and these changes are linked to changes in economic and social circumstances. Moreover, political policies working within changing economic and social conditions can help to produce a consensus where, a short time before, that might have been regarded as impossible.

It does not seem, then, that there is much enlightenment in the proposition that democracies will work effectively only if 'fundamental' principles are not politically unchallenged. This is to fail to take account of the great complexity of the influences that affect the formulation and operation of interests within a democratic society.

As noted before, it is necessary to distinguish two different situations. To preserve their authority and support, political regimes (and not only democratic regimes) must avoid interferences with interests which would provoke more than an acceptable level of opposition. That is, they must avoid provoking a negative consensus. This sort of situation (which may be said to contribute to the toleration of the regime and its policies) is to be distinguished from the other, in which the authority or legitimacy of the regime is *positively* supported by some form of consensus.

As for the first type of situation, a very large part of the existing arrangements of a stable society is maintained by widespread acceptance or support in the community and these arrangements are not always aspects of established social living that a political theorist might classify as 'fundamental'. Many are, of course; for example, many types of liberty customarily enjoyed by members of the community, many of the rights and usages concerned with the institution of the family, rights and traditions connected with religious practice. Democratic states have often run into difficulty when they have attempted to interfere with perhaps less 'fundamental' matters of popular habit and sentiment. An example often quoted is the American experience with prohibition of the sale of alcohol; similarly, efforts to ration goods or to establish price controls have usually encountered a great deal of opposition and evasion. Of course, the intensity and breadth of popular support for such well-established parts of the pattern of social living are different in different countries. It is, however, true that in all modern countries a great portion of the existing social system is maintained by popular attitude and sentiment of considerable intensity and political leaders who wish to preserve democratic processes refrain from 'questioning' them. Governments adopt a policy of non-interference, either because interference would engender an undesirable volume of opposition or because it is thought that legislation would be insufficiently enforceable: the amount of evasion of the law to be expected (together perhaps with consequential disadvantages) makes the legislation imprudent.

The stance of non-interference is, of course, directed not only towards aspects of social living which enjoy something approaching consensual support. There are also, at any given time, specialized or minority interests and established practices that governments and major political parties will respect and leave alone. It is unlikely that any government in a contemporary industrialized democracy would attempt to legislate, or that any political party would propose, that trade unions should be made illegal, or the profession of Catholic religious belief forbidden; no party, that is, that seriously intended to preserve democratic forms of government. Governments are compelled to take account of the location and distribution of power in a society, and to refrain from attacking interests of

A

minority groups where such an attack would probably provoke a level of resistance and social disturbance judged to be unacceptable. There is here an important difference between the capabilities of a democratic political regime and a non-democratic regime. A Hitler could suppress the trade unions, destroy the freedom of workers to seek employment where they wished, and imprison outspoken leaders of religious communities because he was willing to use the force and repression necessary. A political leadership committed to the preservation of democratic norms is subject to many constraints from which the non-democratic regime is free. After all, a democratic regime pursues social stability as one of its objectives because those who operate it know that *social* stability is one of the conditions of the stability of the democratic order.

But if we consider further those cases in which democratic governments 'respect' established powerful minorities, there is more to be said. There are no doubt many cases in which governments, or all leading political parties, 'respect' interests and demands of a minority even though it is very doubtful whether those demands would be endorsed by the majority. And this is not always because of the powers of opposition and resistance those minorities could bring into play; it is more often a matter of the identical electoral calculations of rival political parties. It seems that in some democratic societies religious minorities enjoy 'power of veto' in such matters as censorship, the advertising of contraceptives, or aspects of the conduct of public school systems.

We must also, however, note another very important case: that where, although the interests which parties 'respect' and do not question are the interests of a perhaps powerful minority, those interests would, if attacked, be supported by a very large part of the public. There may be a latent consensus which would be brought into life by any political proposal to interfere with the rights or interests in question. In many democratic societies this is perhaps true of the rights of small religious minorities (in Australia, during the last war, the banning of the Jehovah's Witnesses, while it can scarcely be said to have demonstrated the existence under war-time conditions of a consensus in their support, nevertheless brought forth expressions of support that would never have been forthcoming if the sect had not been banned). It is probably also true as regards the making illegal of trade unions; in spite of a great deal of opposition to or irritation with much trade-union activity, it is almost certain that in contemporary democracies an attempt to dissolve trade unions, or even seriously to curtail their established functions and modes of operation, would demonstrate the presence of a quite considerable consensus supporting their existence as economic, social and political institutions. The same is probably also the case regarding much of the structure and practice of modern 'capitalist' industry. And, if it is true, we may say that this sort of consensus, which exists as part of the economic and social structure and which may be latent most of the time, illustrates one important sense in which the stability and effectiveness of a democratic system is connected with consensus. Democratic regimes may expect to be stable to the extent to which they —and the political parties they embody—work within the limits and constraints imposed by existing bodies of social consensus. To some extent they derive authority from their congruence with those bodies. (This is only to detail further a point made by R. A. Dahl in the passage cited in the last chapter.)

The trade-union example is interesting for another reason: it illustrates a manner in which social consensus grows. Initially, in thinking about the meaning of consensus, we may be tempted to contrast consensus with power, with interests in conflict supported by force. In fact, however, consensus often emerges as a result of the use of force or as the result of the growth of an equilibrium of conflicting forces. That successful force can sometimes generate consensus (given sufficient time) is readily enough recognized in the case of regimes that have originally established themselves by violence. It is less often seen to be the case with regard to the social or economic structure of a community. In most industrial countries the growth of trade unions was accompanied by considerable employment of power and force. Governments resisted the growth of their functions and powers by legislation of sometimes extreme penal severity; employers and others often resorted to non-legal violence or intimidation. Trade unionists made use of the strike, and, on occasions, a great deal of intimidation. The trade unions, as their organization improved, and because of the economic functions of the industrial work force and the vulnerability of the economy to strikes, were able to bring considerable power to bear from time to time. This was an area of social conflict which many believed, late in the last century and in the early years of this, would be a permanent and increasingly serious source of disruption or instability for modern industrial society. But industrial society has been compelled, or has found it to be in its interests, to absorb and accommodate itself to trade unions. And now, within this area of actual and potential conflict, there exists a very considerable measure of social consensus. Trade unions as such, and a great part of their established functions and practices, have become part of the generally acknowledged structure of an industrial democratic society; so much so that members of democracies, who are not particularly partisans of trade unions or many of their policies, will cite the lack of independence of trade unions in the Soviet Union as one of the undemocratic characteristics of that country.

This is not to say that issues concerning the organization and activities of unions no longer arise within the political affairs of modern societies (the British General Strike of 1926 and the Trades Disputes Act of 1927 are examples of how attitudes can change and old issues flare into life); but we can say that this example illustrates how an area of social organization once the arena of quite intense conflict can be limited and to some extent 'pacified' by the slow emergence of a social consensus. In this case, it is a consensus that has served to narrow and damp down one intense form of conflict that threatened to impose extreme stresses on the democratic system.

This example suggests that the stability of a democratic regime will be assisted, not so much (or not merely) as Mill suggests if certain fundamental principles or interests are *permanently* the object of social agreement, permanently uncontested in political struggles, but if a society exhibits a capacity to create consensus progressively as a resolution of conflicts about 'fundamental' claims. In the case of trade unions, the century-long conflicts went on partly within the political arena and were partly dealt with by political policy and legislation, and partly within the economic and social systems, outside the arena of political settlement. No doubt, in this particular case, political action (including the attainment by the industrial working class of political rights and organization) contributed a great deal to the general recognition of trade unionism as an institution. But it is not always the case that the growth of social consensus, that in the long run contributes heavily to political stability, reflects itself so strongly in political struggle as in the example of the rise of the trade unions. It is not always true, either, that the continued manifestation of might or the power to maintain a fight has been necessary for an ultimate, widely diffused acceptance of right. It *has* often been true historically; and it has also often been true that powerlessness has prevented a group from influencing the moral or ideological consensus of the community. While it is true that 'value consensus' and power are often intertwined, and that power strong enough to compel others to reckon with it has often been the midwife of consensus, there have been other consensus-making processes that should not be overlooked.

The history of those countries which have developed the most stable systems of democratic institutions during the past century suggests that the mechanism just described has been accompanied by another, a process of peaceful diffusion of ideological or moral assumption and conviction. In the history of the Western democracies, one can discern a process whereby values, rights, ways of living, 'conditions of the good life', already enjoyed by more privileged minorities, are extended and acknowledged to apply to all or most members of the community. The sort of contrast suggested here is that between the assumptions made by the majority of educated Englishmen in the first half of the nineteenth century concerning the legitimate expectations and modes of living of the respectable lower orders (the ethic of 'my station and its duties')—assumptions made, for example, about the sort of education fitting for their children—with the assumptions about such things that now prevail. The process has been one in which moralities of class and status have given ground to moralities and ideologies conceived of as being universally applicable: first as regards the extension of political rights and later the extension of economic and social rights and values. So far as England is concerned, the process has been examined in some detail by T. H. Marshall in *Citizenship and Social Class*. It is one characterized by the evolution of conceptions of common goods, conceptions of objectives and conditions of the good life that apply to all members of a community; a social ethic perhaps adumbrated three centuries before its time by Colonel Rainborough in the Putney Debates with his 'the poorest he that is in England hath a life to live as the greatest he'.

This process of diffusion has no doubt been assisted by many social forces; political forces such as the expanding political rights and activity of the working-class movement; and economic and social development. Obviously, industrial expansion, by alleviating scarcity, has made it possible for other social classes to be admitted more to the enjoyment of 'values' earlier enjoyed by a small minority. Again the technological industrial changes which have created a demand for a different type of working force have had a deep effect on older assumptions about the way of life appropriate for women, and about the rights of children to educational opportunities. Of course social and political morality is not unconnected with a society's institutional structures. However, questions of historical causation are not relevant to our present purposes: the relevant point is that in the Western countries the development of democratic political institutions has been accompanied by the common recognition of important goals or values of life as being themselves common or universally applicable.

This has not led, of course, to anything approaching an equal distribution in any society of the goods or values accepted as being common goods. Nevertheless, it has undoubtedly been a very important factor in contributing to the stability of twentieth-century industrial democracies. It has lowered ideological barriers in these societies and, with the spread of education and therefore understanding and articulateness, with the development of the mass media and other communication facilities, bodies of belief and constellations of interests and demands have come to interact in a single intellectual or ideological market. In particular, the members of contemporary societies have come to talk a common social-moral political language. There is a large measure of consensus at least at a general level concerning the sorts of claims or demands that are legitimate. There can still be minorities not admitted to this common 'moral community' (for example, some racial minorities such as the American Negroes). Social and political conflict is always present in relation to the allocation of 'goods' within the community, and about the speed at which objectives are pursued. Yet, even so, consensus of a very general sort about legitimate goals, claims and expectations makes collaborative political activity possible within a common political system. It is probable that, so far as the political attitudes of the majority of members of contemporary political societies are concerned, the notion of social development, and of the *progressive* achievement of objectives, is an extremely important one and the word 'expectations' plays a very prominent role. It seems, indeed, that the beliefs, assumptions or attitudes of contemporary political man are shaped within the context of a continuously changing and improving society. It is now commonly assumed by students of political systems (of underdeveloped as well as developed systems) that the frustration of widely established though not yet widely achieved expectations can be one of the forces most disruptive of political stability. This suggests that consensus about values or about legitimate claims and expectations applicable to all (or most) members of a community, which has emerged in differing degrees in Western industrial societies over the last one hundred years, has been an important condition of the stability of democratic forms of government.

Political scientists have, of course, been interested in the relation between economic growth and the working of democratic institutions.[4] In the earlier phases of Western industrialization, it may have seemed it would produce economic and social conflict of such magnitude that democratic processes could not cope with it. There was much plausibility in Marx's analysis of the character of capitalist society and the function of the capitalist state. To a considerable extent economic development relieved the pressures; and this was accompanied by the process on which we have been concentrating —the very rapid changes of ideological and moral attitudes which made possible the emergence of a more cohesive political and moral community. These two processes together have, then, contributed to the appearance of a consensus of a very broad kind: a consensus that the general criteria of social and political policy should be a steady, progressive improvement of the 'material' condition of the population and of aspects of their lives connected with 'material' welfare. This consensus has provided a framework within which a shared or common political life could be carried on.

The wide acceptance of such objectives, general as they may be, has provided an element of coherence in the politics of most of the democratic countries. (In some countries, it has, of course, been cut across by particular forms of conflict—racial, religious, linguistic, and, in some developing countries, tribal.) For political leaders and parties, these common objectives provide a considerable area of common ground and make possible a large measure of coherence and continuity in policy and legislation. Continuity in the policies of successive governments, the willingness of a government in most cases to accept and build up the legislation of its predecessors, not to cancel it, is one of the things we mean by political stability. Where there is a fair measure of this type of consensus, the stakes of party competition are in most cases not very great; the loss of what has already been gained is not often threatened; because there is continuity and development, there is always the hope that a defeated party will have the chance later to resume its own programme.

There is one more point to be made. A state of consensus does not *always* imply uniformity of beliefs, goals, interests or expectations. Balfour's remark about the British people 'being so fundamentally at one' could mislead. We have argued that there are some goals and criteria of policy that are shared by the majority of a community, although at any particular time different people interpret them rather differently. There may be considerable diversity within limits adumbrated by the consensus. But as the discussion of the trade-union example may have suggested, there can also be a shared acceptance or 'allowance' of a highly diversified structure of rights, forms of organization, modes of action, ways of life; a general acknowledgement of a distribution of powers, duties, responsibilities, rewards, etc., which in fact in all societies is greatly diversified and unequal. Thus—to return again to Friedrich's criticism of the 'agreement about fundamentals' view— the existence of consensus is not at all necessarily incompatible with a highly pluralistic society.

We have pointed to a few examples of types of consensus that are significant in the stable organization of a democratic political system. We shall go on to examine another possible area of consensus. But first let us return briefly to an earlier question. We have mentioned the opposition sometimes drawn between 'consensus models' and 'conflict models'. Those who adopt 'conflict models' stress the role of power, constraint or coercion in the maintenance of stable social systems; those who adopt (or who are accused of adopting) 'consensus models' seem to minimize the role of power and tend to emphasize rather stability or equilibrium connected with the existence of agreement about common value systems and sets of social norms. In the light of the ground covered in the last few pages we may now make some comments on this opposition.

Those who present 'conflict models' (which usually derive from Marx's theses) distinguish a level of social organization in which stable integration is connected with the operation of common systems of values and norms. But 'below' this level (or, at least, analytically distinguishable from it) is a factual level of social interaction, an infrastructure, in which activities, and interests connected with activities, conflict. These conflicts are usually connected with the unequal allocation of scarce 'goods' and thus with struggles connected with unequal allocation. Within this infrastructure there is no consensus on a common value system, or, at any rate, what common value system there may be is not adequate to reconcile the conflicting interests. Therefore this is an area in which power and constraint operate to establish or maintain a balance of forces and demands—so far, that is, as a balance is maintained, because it is also often asserted that from this infrastructure is generated the dynamism responsible for social change. In any case, it is argued that this is a level of social organization at which consensus about norms, principles or objectives cannot be posited as the chief or even an important condition of equilibrium or stability; in so far as stability can be found, it is to be attributed to other mechanisms, and especially to power, coercion or constraint, or to the existence of balances of conflicting forces.[5]

In dealing with arguments between 'consensus' and 'conflict' theorists, the main difficulty is to discover at what points the two models are opposed. No one will deny the existence of conflict (and of power or coercion) as ingredients in the structure of any complex and highly differentiated society; it is equally difficult to deny the existence within relatively stable societies of various forms of consensus. The main problem is to trace how consensus and conflict, consensus and power, are interrelated. We have suggested numerous interrelations. For example, it would not be tenable to assume a stark opposition between 'interests' and 'values' because definitions of 'legitimate interests' or claims come to be widely accepted as a result of consensus about values, but this is not to say that all the interests and claims insisted upon by one social group are commonly recognized interests and claims: the fact that political activity goes on shows that this is not so.

Again, we have insisted both that in important instances consensus arises as the result of effectively exercised power or pressure, and also that, even without consensus, stable social arrangements or accommodations arise from a balance of conflicting pressures. These accommodations may either be acknowledged in political policies and in legislation or they may establish themselves *de facto*. The exercise of superior power, enforced compliance, challenges to power, all occur in the social life and the politics of all states, but more freely and openly, of course, in democratic states.

Nevertheless, it may still be argued that, if the stability and continuity of the economic system depended wholly or mainly on
balance of force any society would be a much tenser and more
unstable system than it actually is. One could not accept the image
of a democratic society as being a system of mutual deterrence; and,
for that matter, even in the international system where 'balance of
power' and mutual deterrence have played quite important roles,
situations of mutual deterrence work within sets of norms and
understandings which define what the parties can and cannot do.
At least, the more these exist, the more stable and predictable the
situation is. Returning to the domestic society, one would expect
that a system constituted largely of structured conflict would
generate a pervasive attitude of political nervousness, a degree of
mutual distrust, a tendency to be incessantly active in mobilizing
support, a fear of tactical defeat, that would presumably create an
atmosphere very unfavourable to the forms of toleration and
restraint which are central in a democratic polity. And indeed it
does sometimes happen in a democratic country that relations between opposing interests produce just these characteristics. However, the main general point has already been made: it is not a
question of consensus *or* conflict; what is interesting is the inter-
connection between them. That is the position from the sociological
point of view. We might also say, from the point of view of political
philosophy, that the *quality* of democratic life and activity seems
to be connected with the manner in which consensus and conflict
are combined. (That will be the subject of the next chapter.)

Up to this point we have been discussing some examples of
consensus that may exist in relation to the wider system of economic and social institutions, relationships and powers. Let us now
turn to another 'level' at which consensus may or may not exist
and ask whether its existence at this 'level' is in fact necessary for
the stable working of a democratic political order.

This is the 'level' of democratic values, norms, principles, procedures or institutions themselves. Political theorists have often
raised the question whether, in order to have a solidly based
democratic system, a considerable part of the population of the
community must adhere to or support the values or general principles of democracy, and have some degree of commitment to the
essential procedures and institutions of democracy. And some
theorists of democracy have either maintained or assumed that a

fairly common support for democratic values or norms—respect for freedom of speech and organization, tolerance of conflicting opinions, willingness to abide by majority decisions, and so on—is a necessary feature of secure and successful democracy.

Yet this is an extremely complicated question and only a very foolhardy writer would be very positive in his conclusions. In recent years political scientists have made empirical studies of the attitudes of members of democratic societies concerning funda-mental democratic values and norms and we shall shortly refer to their findings. But there is one initial caution to make. There are obviously very great differences among states which have succeeded in maintaining democratic government over fairly long periods of time and, therefore, it is not possible to assert general propositions applicable to all of them. For example, some democratic states (including post-war Italy and France) have powerful parties of the left or right, including Communist parties, which are by doctrine opposed to much of the established liberal-democratic ideology and procedure. These must differ in important ways from other states in which parties hostile to the established constitutional regime are much less important. Again, some democracies, such as the United States, contain ethnic and cultural minorities so violently disaffected with their economic and social situation that one could not assume their allegiance to the existing form of govern-ment. There are states counting as democracies of the Western type where there are regions or economic groups much less inte-grated into the national political and social systems than in other democracies; Italy would be an example of one kind, India of another. Studies such as those by Almond and Verba[6] show that people in different democracies differ considerably in the intensity of their allegiance to or estrangement from their own political systems and politicians. One conclusion, it seems, is that countries which maintain democratic structures and processes of a kind can exhibit wide variation with respect to their knowledge of or attitudes towards values, principles and practices of democratic politics and government.[7]

Political scientists who have studied, by sample and survey, popular attitudes towards democratic values and institutions (mainly in the United States) have tended to come to common conclusions which may be summarized as follows:

1 A considerable proportion of the members of the

community have no clear understanding of the concepts, principles and norms of a democratic system. They cannot express the arguments conventionally accepted as justifying democratic procedures. It cannot be claimed, therefore, that their support for a democratic polity derives from rationally based conviction.

2 A large proportion of citizens are confused and equivocal in their attitudes towards democratic ideas and norms. They will often assent to democratic formulas presented in a very general way, but recommend anti-democratic measures in certain concrete situations. Some who profess to accept democratic norms as broad generalities manifest strongly anti-democratic attitudes in special areas of social organization. Examples of this are 'working-class authoritarianism', strongly authoritarian postures in business or industry, intolerance of divergence or dissent in small local communities. Thus, it cannot be claimed that democratic attitudes permeate great modern societies widely or evenly or that they have everywhere permeated deeply.

3 There is the distinction between 'fair-weather democrats' and 'thick and thin democrats': those who give priority to other interests, and support democratic procedures only when they serve interests regarded as being more vital; and those who on almost all occasions defend or choose the democratic way. In modern states, organizations commanding power have frequently brought pressure to bear to resist decisions taken by governments in accord with the established democratic processes.

4 There is the factor of political indifference or apathy. The political concern of a large part of the population is intermittent and marginal at best. So far as many members of the community are concerned, compliance with and occasional participation in processes of democratic government are probably a matter of habit or routine, not of conviction or 'identification with' the activities of government. Indeed, a school of democratic theorists has argued that occasional and low-keyed interest in political affairs, a marginal, intermittent and interest-specific concern with political issues so far as a large part of the community is concerned, is a protection for democratic processes and the tolerances they depend on. It is supposed that overactivity and a too intense concern with political issues can put great strains on

democratic institutions. It may be said that post-war Western theorizing about the nature and conditions of a democratic society has been dominated by pluralistic modes of thinking which discount ideological intensity and unity in their models of a democratic system and which emphasize instead the diversity of interests which are loosely aggregated and accommodated to each other through the operation of political processes. This is to regard governments (and systems of government) mainly from an instrumental point of view; perhaps it implies that the strength of a democratic form of government mainly depends on its capacity to continue to satisfy the expectations of most citizens.

5   There is still another argument, explicit or implicit in a great deal of contemporary theorizing, that casts doubt on the existence of a true consensus supporting democracy. It is the argument that, even if we consider only the more articulate exponents of democratic creeds, there is no agreement about what democratic values are, or what are the institutional arrangements needed to embody them. There are competing conceptions of what democracy is or requires; important differences concerning the weight to be given to majority rule *versus* minority rights, to direct participation in political decision making *versus* processes of representation, to formal equality of political rights *versus* greater equality in economic conditions or greater provision for economic security. Within the comparatively recent history of democratic ideology and practice such shifts of emphasis have clearly occurred; all Western democracies have become less 'liberal' in the older individualistic sense and more concerned about 'freedoms from' —about forms of security. In this way the democratic ideology itself is characterized by a considerable degree of incoherence, and these conceptual incoherences are linked with differences of values and goals in the political attitudes and behaviour of members of the democratic society.

Moreover, no state exists, however democratic, in which the forms of politics and government are determined solely by the end of achieving democratic values. At the best, values and norms of democracy are only one set of considerations that affect the shape of political institutions. The form and working of actual institutions are also shaped by other pressures. For example, much of the elaborate bureaucratic machinery of the contemporary industrialized democracies was created largely by pressure of circumstances, by the nature of the tasks imposed on the government of very complex societies; and it is arguable what the significance of a highly developed bureaucracy is for some of the norms of democracy. Much of the new institutional structures that have established themselves centrally in contemporary industrial democratic states would be supported by other than strictly democratic values—by the desirability of a high level of efficiency and rationality in decision making, for example, for the need to concentrate leadership and authority. Thus, some democracies have developed political parties which demand a high measure of centralized discipline and unity. These party machines exercise considerable control over the selection of electoral candidates and so over the operation of a large part of the political machinery. And party discipline and solidarity have been, in some countries, main factors in the steadily growing ascendancy of the executive over the legislature. These institutional developments many members of contemporary states would defend—but not necessarily because they assist in the fuller achievement of democratic values. On the contrary, there are many others whose conception of democracy is such that they maintain that developments of the sort just mentioned are in fact unfavourable for the achievement of democratic values.

The point is, then, that we find in any highly complicated democratic society diverging conceptions of what democracy is and what it requires and conflicting views concerning the relation of much of the existing political and administrative machinery to democratic ideas. And we find also other values, distinct from democratic values, to which different sections of the community will adhere with different degrees of attachment. To put it mildly, the value systems of modern democratic societies are extremely complex and certainly not free from ambiguities, tensions and contradictions. If we take all these facts into account, we must conclude that it would be a very bold assumption to make that the strength of a democratic system rests upon a consensus in support of the values and norms of democracy, if by that we mean a positive attachment to those values and norms manifested by a very large part of the citizen body. It would certainly be very difficult to demonstrate the existence of such a consensus, to show that the conception of a 'common value system' (of the sort we are now considering) has its empirical equivalent. It seems, indeed, that there may be a great deal of truth in the contention of Shils and many others that the incoherences and tensions in the political values *professed* by different members of a community do not lead to more social and political friction than they normally do only because the attitudes that most people have to the values they profess are in most cases of rather low intensity. Most people, most of the time, do not strongly insist on ideological consistency nor on faithfulness to some one particular set of values; thus the ambiguities, contradictions and compromises are accommodated without too much strain. In this sense tolerance is clearly a mark of democracy; but it is an open question to what extent (in a particular society) the existence of such tolerance is due to a commitment to tolerance as a value, and to what extent it is due to some of the many other circumstances which can lead to the acceptance in practice of compromises and contradictions.

In any case, it would seem implausible to describe or explain the state of affairs we have been describing in terms of consensus, the general adherence to a *common* value system. What we appear to find in any complex society, and in an 'open' or democratic society more than in others, is a patchwork of political and social arrangements, related in turn to a patchwork of divergent and loosely adjusted values, norms and objectives. And it is gratuitous to assume that any single individual, group or class, and still less *all* members of the community, either 'will' or actively support the patchwork that happens to exist, although the great majority of them no doubt are willing enough to tolerate the greater part of it.

Of course, to describe the stability of a democracy at the level of the value system that exists is not necessarily to praise or recommend it. In most circumstances perhaps stability is itself a value. But many will argue that the relative absence of opposition and conflict, and a general toleration of ambiguity, equivocation, contradiction and easy accommodation, are themselves anti-democratic characteristics which limit democratic activities, or which are connected with a low level of political energy and participation. Some critics of contemporary democratic societies speak about their 'hypocrisy'; it seems that they have partly in mind just these juxtapositions of divergent values and the accommodations between them. These critics are apt to complain about the enervating effects of 'consensus politics'. In view of what has just been said, this may appear a misleading diagnosis. On the one hand, the critics themselves often seem to desire a condition of still greater consensus: a condition of society in which one particular conception of democracy or one particular set of democratic values are more generally and more intensely supported. On the other hand, while there are elements or components of consensus to be identified in any stable democratic state, it cannot be assumed that the stability of those states is to be attributed to a general or nearly unanimous consensus about a common value system.

There is another important and frequently asserted hypothesis on this question. It is the contention that within the type of democratic societies we have in mind there is invariably a wider, more articulate and more strongly felt consensus about basic values and 'rules of the game' among the political 'élites' and 'influentials' than among the rank and file. It is sometimes also asserted that a high level of consensus among 'élites' is a necessary condition for the relatively stable, peaceful working of the democratic machinery. This is the point at which consensus is supposedly especially important.

Who counts as 'élite'? Sometimes 'élite' is identified with 'more articulate': those who are more politically and socially articulate are likely to be more in agreement in their support for basic values, for central institutions and rules of the game, than the less articulate. Empirically this may be so in most modern democracies most of the time. The majority of the articulate may well in the course of their education have become highly 'socialized'—trained to absorb the values of the *status quo*. Also, of course, it may well be that the great majority of the articulate have strong interests that attach them to established values, institutions and arrangements. Nor will it be denied that it is serious for a political system when substantial sections of the articulate become disaffected from existing society; their very capacity to articulate and communicate, often to organize, can obviously make them serious irritants in the body politic. As rough generalizations these are truisms. Even so, we must resist the tendency to exaggerate consensus: there always exist segments of the articulate or intelligentsia who are bearers of values antagonistic to dominant political, economic, social or moral values.

We may take 'élite' in a more limited sense: as comprising those especially who are most influential in controlling or operating the political parties, the organs of government (including the legal institutions and the civil services), and the other organizations which are central in the working of the political system—for example, industrial organizations, the trade unions, the great professional associations, the powerful, organized interest groups. In short, we may equate the 'élite' more or less with what Mosca called 'the ruling class'. And in estimating the components of consensus and its general role in the cohesion or stability of a political society, it is certainly true that a study of the ruling class is extremely important. The internal relations of this 'class', its relations to the rest of society, are critical for the presence and absence of consensus.

It is clearly broadly true that those who may be said to operate the democratic system can be expected to be more attached to its values, more consciously concerned with observing and guarding the rules of the game, than most other members of the political public. Modern democracies are dominated to a considerable degree by two or a very few organized political parties. They operate the system in many important ways: they control the processes of selection and representation, they manage the legislatures, they control the executive, they enjoy not an exclusive but a very special role in the formulation of issues and policies. They are both parts of the system and products of it: they are quite thoroughly integrated into it. It is hard to see how the 'major' parties could not both by profession and practice maintain the 'rules of the game'. As Robert de Jouvenel is said to have remarked of the politics of the Third French Republic: 'There is more in common between two deputies only one of whom is a revolutionary than there is between two revolutionaries only one of whom is a deputy.' This quip hints at a fundamental characteristic of modern democratic party systems.

Acceptance of the norms, the rules, the machinery, naturally tends to flow from leaders to led. Inevitably the political thinking and sentiments of the rank and file flow into the channels provided by the organizations that mobilize them. Where two or three parties control the working of the political system, it is always difficult for beliefs, demands and issues which the major parties decline to take up to find effective expression in political life: not impossible but especially difficult. It is hard to estimate the significance of this, but it does appear that a stable and highly organized party system tends to channel and constrict to some degree the tendencies of opinion and demand that can exert influence on policy and action. And, if the parties which possess so much control over the working of all parts of the political machinery are much at one in supporting the existing rules of the game, and largely agree in beliefs about values and policies, it is not to be expected that many members of the community will have the means to develop a critical and independent stance, still less be able to express it. The example of the political parties and other sections of the political 'élites' strengthens the disposition inherent in most people to conform to the familiar existing forms of procedure as being natural or perhaps inevitable.

Thus some components of the prevailing consensus on which the system depends will be the products of pressures exerted by dominant institutions and élites: the system itself plays a part in the manufacture of attitudes and habits required for its own survival. Elements of consensus are implanted and consolidated by the downward pressures of institutional practice. Of course in any democratic state there is a very complex pattern of interacting causes and influences; and for any particular society the components of consensus and dissensus, and the social forces responsible for each of them, have to be analysed in their own terms. Not much can be said about these matters which is equally applicable to all democracies. If we consider, for example, the dominant political parties in different democracies, we observe different forms and degrees of consensus between them with respect to shared support for basic constitutional principles and rules, or ultimate values; in the history of the one country important disagreements arise between the central parties about constitutional issues. The authority that dominant institutions and élites command partly depends on their willingness and ability to satisfy expectations of powerful interests and groups which may in turn be supported by areas of strong social consensus. And it is also often true that there are important forms of consensus—strong attachments to certain common values—which remain latent or unexpressed for very long periods, and which declare themselves and rally to the support of established norms and institutions only when they are threatened or attacked. In ordinary times of political peace and quiet, it is not easy to determine how firmly if at all allegiance to democratic norms and values is part of the constitution of the democratic citizens; what at least is certain is that it is not a requirement for the peaceful working of a democratic system that citizens should wear their ideological hearts upon their sleeves.

In an article quoted at the beginning of this chapter H. J. McClosky asserts: 'The opinion has long prevailed that consensus is needed to achieve stability, but the reverse may be the correct formulation; that is, that so long as conditions remain stable, consensus is not required; it becomes essential only when conditions are disorganised.' For so-called consensus theorists that is of course a paradox. McClosky is asserting that there are conditions not connected with value-consensus or norm-consensus which may be sufficient to preserve the stability of a society; and that consensus may only be important when these conditions fail to work. Thus, a society which encountered severe economic depression and dislocation might escape political conflict and violence if strong agreement about values and symbols preserved a sense of national unity, or if there were strong attachment to existing democratic values and norms. In fact, it was often asserted during the 1930s that for reasons such as these depression would not bring about the success of a Fascist revolution in Britain as it had done in Germany and other countries.

McClosky is right to emphasize the importance of non-consensual conditions of stability. But it would seem to follow from the argument of this chapter that he is wrong in suggesting that stability—or at least the stability of democratic processes—can exist independently of consensus, for we have set out some reasons for believing that a democratic system is unlikely to work very successfully without the support of certain forms and some measure of consensus. We have tried to point to some of the forms of consensus that may well be important conditions of a stable democracy, and to others that seem less likely to be. But we have also emphasized that democracies differ in these respects; that there are no uniformities or generalizations assertable of all of them; that each more or less stable democracy is likely to exhibit its own pattern of consensual and non-consensual forces.

6/Consensus, Dissent and Ideology

Whatever else may be said about consensus, one proposition is certain: there is no consensus among social theorists concerning the political role or significance of consensus itself. There are flatly contradictory views. That democracy requires consensus is probably the formulation that the majority of political scientists now support. But, as we have noted, some contend that consensus may, in certain circumstances, be unfavourable to the existence or vigour of democratic procedures or ways of life.

Democracy requires consensus: our discussion should have suggested that this generalization is unilluminating and misleading. In some senses the proposition is a truism: obviously, no democratic political system (no other type of political system for that matter) can be expected to work effectively without a considerable measure of consensus. But these always exists also a considerable amount of dissensus. One conclusion we would draw is that is unlikely that there are any generalizations that are true and informative of all political systems, or even of all democracies. In the analysis of the stability and instability of particular societies, we can identify types and areas of agreement, and we can say how these operate in order to strengthen the processes of politics and government. We can also identify areas of disagreement and conflict, and try to see how these are contained within limits so that they do not weaken the authority or effectiveness of political institutions. But there seems to be no prospect of our being able to say that consensus of this or that kind is a *necessary* condition of political stability.

It is arguable that, for the stability of democratic systems, some types of consensus are more important than others. It may be that a general agreement with, or support for, the basic constitutional rules and the structure of political rights associated with them are more important than consensus about particular issues of policy, or particular moral codes. Such a contention was examined in the last chapter, and we saw that even this hypothesis has its difficulties. Even so far as basic 'rules', values, and conceptions of political organization are concerned, the actual condition of any modern democratic state appears to fall a great deal short of consensus. Again, it may sometimes be misleading to say that consensus about fundamental constitutional values and rules is always more important than consensus about issues of policy; it is not hard to imagine circumstances in which intense conflict about some issue of policy (for example, a government's policy with regard to industrial wages in a period of economic depression) could shake the stability of a society as much as disagreement about some part of the established constitutional system. Societies, especially democratically organized societies, could be highly vulnerable at different 'levels' of social organization, and not only at the political or constitutional level.

Moreover, as we have noted, compliance with the fundamental constitutional values, rules and procedures is by no means wholly a matter of consensus in any very strict sense: inertia, indifference, habituation, a relatively unthinking conformity with practices and norms supported by élites and authorities all form part of the social state we call stability. And another point connected with this, which is important although we have not chosen to emphasize it, is that generalizations about the roles of consensus and dissensus (or conflict) are particularly unilluminating because of our inability to speak precisely about degrees of stability, consensus or dissensus. It has been fundamental to our argument that when we speak both of consent and consensus we are speaking of *continua*: of a scale of motives and attitudes that shade off insensibly into others that we would not attribute to the sphere of consent or consensus. And consent and consensus can, of course, be measured in terms of more than one dimension. We can enquire about the proportion of the members of a community who share in a given consensus, and also about the intensity with which the individual members of a consensus group, or distinguishable sectors of the consensus group, support whatever is supposed to be the object of the consensus.

Now, it is an empirical fact that in the case of consensus concerning virtually any object or set of objects in an actual democratic society, whether it be consensus about basic values or rules of the game or norms, there is present an exceedingly complicated and confused pattern of attitudes and motives manifested by different individuals and different sections of the consensus group. It makes sense to ask: How wide or how strong is the consensus? in any particular case; but it is not easy to see how the question can be answered, except in an extremely impressionistic way. We can attempt analyses of and judgements about the measure of consensus present in some particular context in some particular society at a particular time. Without expecting any very exact result, we can make use of a number of available instruments of social observation and judgement. But when we become more ambitious and try to formulate generalizations about societies, laws concerning regular connections, our task is an impossible one. In reply to the assertion 'Democracy requires consensus', we may reply, not merely 'What kind of consensus?', but also, 'What measure of consensus?' or 'How strong a consensus of that kind?' These are questions that no one can answer; difficulties that are quite fundamental in any attempt to produce something that may be called 'consensus theory'. As we have tried to show, the condition of compliance, conformity or stability that may characterize a society is compounded of so many attitudes, motives and forms of behaviour, most of which are capable of ranging over so many different shades of quality and degrees of intensity, that the general assertion that democracy (or stability) requires consensus tells us very little indeed if we cannot be a great deal more specific with respect to kind and degree. Even the narrower assertion that democracy requires consensus about certain classes of values or norms or rules of the game is, for the same reason, not greatly informative. This says little more than that consensual elements are a necessary part of the complex web that supports stable society or stable democracy.

Although we have not chosen to emphasize the point, the problem becomes still more difficult if what we are asserting is a regular connection between consensus and stability. Political stability is also a state that admits of great and important differences of kind and degree. There have been democratic states in the modern world that have been, comparatively speaking, highly stable, e.g. Britain, the United States, the Scandinavian democracies and the older British Commonwealth countries. Others, for example France and Weimar Germany, have been relatively unstable. Some democratic states have persisted for a long time despite the presence of forces making for instability. France is perhaps the most important example. Forces conducive to instability include, for example, large, organized political parties actively opposed to the constitutionally established political system, or minorities of significant size (such as many American Negroes) so discontented that their allegiance to the constitutionally established political system can hardly be assumed. There have been democracies which have contained classes or social groups whose interests have been so little integrated into the prevailing structures of policy and government that they have created a continuous threat of political instability. But many of these countries have preserved a measure of stability (in the sense that their system of democratic political institutions has survived and operated with a sufficient degree of effectiveness) for long periods in spite of a considerable amount of opposition, disaffection and dissensus. So, because 'instability' is a highly indeterminate concept also, general propositions that assert a direct link between consensus and stability are bound to involve radical oversimplification.

In saying all this, of course, we do not intend to deny that consensus is an important concept or that the analysis of existing areas of consensus is an important and necessary part of the analysis of the stability of societies and political systems. The objection is simply to the assertion of quite general theoretical hypotheses concerning uniform connections between consensus and stability (or integration), and against the presentation of oversimplified and exclusive 'consensus models' for the explanation of social integration. (Equally objectionable, of course, are the 'conflict models' and 'coercion models' advanced for the same purpose.) It seems clear enough that, when we try to analyse the conditions sufficient or necessary for the persistence and continuity of on-going political and social systems, we are dealing with situations involving a very large number of causally important variables; and such variables as consensus and conflict, coercion, power and 'free' or voluntary compliance, are intertwined with one another in exceedingly complicated ways.

In what has so far been said in this, as well as in the two preceding chapters, we have been considering consensus exclusively as a term of sociological analysis and explanation. But it is also a term of social philosophy. We began this book with some discussion of the long-standing doctrine that no political authority can be morally defensible if, in some sense, it does not possess or exercise its authority with the consent of the governed. We also noted that many political theorists have believed that government with the consent of the governed is one necessary characteristic of a free or democratic political community. (We shall need to return to this doctrine later in this chapter.) Many political thinkers have also held that what is true of consent is true also of consensus: that the more truly it can be said that the political system or system of government, and the policies followed by governments, are supported by a consensus on the part of the members of the community, the more—so far as that goes—will the state be a free and democratic state. We say 'so far as that goes': few liberal-democratic theorists of democracy will say that a high level of consensus is a *sufficient* condition of a free or democratic state since that would, in principle, require us to admit that a highly authoritarian or dictatorial form of state might be a very free or democratic one. Many do, however, believe that it is a *necessary* condition, so that, 'other things being equal', the greater the consensus supporting the regime and its policies, the greater the measure of democracy. This is so since, although consensus may often not meet the more stringent conditions required by some political theorists before they will acknowledge the existence of consent, still the presence of supporting or permissive consensus is assumed to imply the absence of coercion and constraint.

There is, however, another, opposing, view, and perhaps we can most conveniently look at some of the more philosophical questions concerning the connections between consensus and democracy by starting with it. This is the view which has been rather often expressed in recent years (and which we have already encountered in the passage quoted from Professor Friedrich) that 'too much' of the wrong kind of consensus can lower the level and impair the quality of democratic activity. The argument is a very simple one: the spread of consensus implies the weakening of opposition, the dying down of the fertile clash between different beliefs, aspirations, interests and ways of living. Consensus means that society becomes increasingly uniform or homogenized. Democracy, it is assumed, requires diversity of beliefs and goals and open contest between individuals and groups identified with them. It requires active competition and opposition.

What is involved here are not simply different views about the role of consensus in the support of a democratic system, but also different notions of the nature of democracy in action. On this more philosophical level of discussion, Marxists, or those who have defended the reality of Soviet democracy, have argued that systems of opposing and competing political parties are not necessary, nor do they have a basis for existing, in a classless society. Their claim is that where there is so great an identity of interests, so inclusive and profound a consensus, 'disagreement about fundamentals' does not exist. In this sense, Marxists are 'consensus theorists' when it is a matter of explaining and justifying 'Soviet democracy'. Many of them have also argued (it is the classical Leninist argument) that capitalist democracies have only been able to operate peacefully or with stability because there has existed, not a genuine consensus about fundamentals, but a bogus one: in capitalist democracies the fundamentals of economic structure, property distribution and the like have not been permitted to become matters of political struggle. It seems, then that the liberal-democratic theorists of democracy and Leninists have had a theoretical link: assent to the proposition that 'democracy requires consensus'.[1] But there are important differences. The liberal-democratic consensus theorists apparently assume (since, after all, they have usually held that competing political parties and organized and open opposition are *also* necessary mechanisms of any truly democratic order) that democracy requires a *balance* of consensus and dissensus; they must reject both the possibility and the desirability of absolute or complete consensus. The anti-consensus theorists may be said to believe that when the balance swings too far to the side of consensus, democracy is impaired. If we were to compare these three positions in detail, we would find a number of connected differences about the nature and formation of consensus; about the balance of consensus–dissensus required for the best operation of a democratic order; and—arising from the second difference—about what democracy in practice is.

It is often said that the growth or spread of consensus has been a remarkable feature of the history of a number of the Western democracies during the present century and that this has affected the character of political activity in those societies. That evolving consensus is commonly supposed to include the following levels or aspects of political and social life:

1 A consensus concerning the basic constitutional arrangements of the state. In the course of the last hundred years all political classes have been admitted to the enjoyment of the basic political rights; all have equal legal opportunities to participate in political activity; all have the opportunity to exercise political power and to have their demands taken account of. Thus, the great constitutional issues, the struggle about political rights, which have played so central a part in European politics for the last four

centuries, are no longer very active issues: so far as the basic rights and arrangements of the democratic state are concerned, there now exists a very considerable measure of consensus.

2   Again, it is suggested that there now exists a considerable measure of consensus concerning the main goals of social policy and the manner in which they should be pursued. Economic growth, and the steady improvement for all classes of the material conditions of life and other social goods associated with higher standards of living are accepted by the great majority of citizens of advanced democracies as imperatives of social policy.

3   In this connection the concept of the 'welfare state', the state that aims at the achievement of economic and social improvement, and of greater security for all members of the community, through the provision of an assemblage of now generally accepted social services, has come to dominate thinking about the proper ends of government.

4   There is a very wide acceptance of the view that it is the function and duty of the state itself to use its own powers and resources to achieve these goals.

These are some, at least, of the main elements of the consensus that is often said to have evolved within the economically advanced democracies. Within these areas of agreement there is obviously a great deal of room for political disagreement or conflict; nevertheless, it is implied, they provide a framework of general agreement wider and stronger than anything that has existed in Western societies for many centuries.[2]

It is also frequently suggested that the more intensive integration of modern industrialized societies, the increased means of easy communication, and the enormously expanded role of the central political and administrative authorities in the management or support of social affairs have aided the growth of consensus. E. A. Shils writes:

> When, as in modern society, a more unified economic system, a political democracy, urbanization and education have brought the different sectors of the population into more frequent contact with each other and created even greater mutual awareness, the central value system has found a

wider acceptance than in other periods of the history of society ... To a greater extent than ever before in history, the mass of the society in modern Western societies feel themselves to be part of their societies in a way in which their ancestors never did ... They have come to be parts of the civil society with a feeling of attachment to that society and a feeling of moral responsibility for observing its rules and for sharing in its authority.

However, Shils also sees that this more direct and more continuous involvement in the one political and economic system can generate conflicts of a type that might be avoided in a looser, less integrated society: 'None the less this greater incorporation carries with it also an inherent tension. Those who participate in the central institutional and value systems ... also feel their position as outsiders, their remoteness from the centre, in a way in which their forebears probably did not feel it.'[3]

Further, this consensus (or the assumption that it exists) has been one factor encouraging the prevalence of a particular type of view concerning the most rational character and style of democratic politics. The argument is that ideologies and the conflicts of ideologies have become steadily less prominent in the politics of the highly advanced democracies. Democratic politics are seen as no longer concerned with contests between the great 'isms', with highly charged debate about the 'great issues'. The style of political activity which best conforms to the character of highly industrialized democracies, and is made possible by the type and measure of consensus that has in fact emerged in these societies, is considered to be one that devotes itself to the progressive solution of specific problems, the piecemeal amelioration of conditions that cause discontent or suffering, the production of policies that accommodate specific interests and demands: the politics of 'piecemeal engineering' or 'incrementalism'.[4] This is a conception of a style of politics that emphasizes a narrowing of the range of political activity to the progressive forging of adjustments between a large spectrum of relatively specific interests and demands, in contrast with aspirations towards large-scale transformation inspired by 'isms' or ideologies.

This view has been put with great clarity by Robert Dahl in a number of works. He questions the general appropriateness of a two-party system: the circumstances in which it is the optimal solution, he suggests, may be uncommon. 'The typical solution of democracies is not concentration but dispersion, not strict competition but bargaining and coalescent strategies.'[5] We spoke earlier in this chapter of Western theorists of democracy implying that some sort of balance of consensus and dissensus is the optimum situation: Dahl speaks of extensive consensus and dissensus both being unfavourable to rationality and suggests the possibility of a balance between dissent and 'calm and objective appraisal of alternatives'. And he goes on to say: 'To be concerned about the decline of structural oppositions in most Western democracies may well be an anachronism, a throwback to 19th century styles of thought. Should we not begin instead to adjust our minds to the notion that in the future—or at least in the short-run future in which it is not wholly senseless to extrapolate present trends—a great many Western democracies will have rather high levels of agreement and not much structural opposition.'[6]

Now, it is often asserted that this notion of a non-ideological style of politics is itself an ideology, a value-determined preference. No doubt it is; but the point is that the ideology is established or implied by the reigning consensus of the advanced Western democracies, and that therefore this ideology is not itself a political issue. It is the ideological consensus that makes this form of politics, which has much to commend it on other grounds, possible. It is sometimes maintained that one reason it is especially difficult to build democratic institutions and procedures similar to those of contemporary Western states in many of the developing countries of Africa and Asia is that the consensus concerning basic political structures and rights, and about the central goal or imperative of policy, is absent; indeed, since these things are themselves in the process of creation, they are the subject of ideological conflict and part of the substance of day-to-day politics.[7] But it is beyond the scope of this book to discuss the special circumstances of societies in the process of 'modernization'.

We have just been outlining important views about the direction of development of Western democracies, and about the sociological foundations of their political systems. Nor is there any doubt that these views have their ideological or 'justificatory' overtones: Dahl is not the only one who inclines to believe that the emergent style of democratic politics is one that gives greater scope for political 'rationality'. At this late stage in our own discussion, we will not enquire into the empirical truth of these assertions about a growing consensus. We may have reasons for grave doubt: it is very easy *not* to detect the undercurrents of discontent and disaffection in any society organized as modern large-scale industrial societies are. In Dahl's case, our doubts may be raised merely by the fact that, in one place, he classifies the United States as a 'high consensus' society. Just as many Marxists and Leninists have been disposed to detect class domination everywhere, so many contemporary political sociologists, preoccupied with questions of social integration, stability, systems analysis, tend to see consensus in places where others might well see mainly cracks and strains. However, we have said all we wish to say about these issues of empirical interpretation. Let us return to our more philosophical concern: How are 'high' and 'low' consensus related to the existence of political freedom and democratic activity?

Towards the end of *Political Opposition in Western Democracies* Dahl himself poses the question that troubles many contemporary students of Western society and theorists of democracy. 'That a large number of democracies have won the battle for allegiance among all social strata is, surely, a satisfying victory to anyone who believes in the values of a democratic polity. Yet it is difficult to avoid the sense of disquiet that follows hard upon one's awareness that severe criticism of social and economic structures has all but disappeared from the political life of many Western democracies— or else has become a monopoly of political forces like the communists and the radical Right whose allegiance to democratic values is, to say the least, doubtful.' (p. 398). Perhaps the assumption about the facts has been weakened since Dahl wrote (1966). But the theoretical question remains: Why should it be possible to hold, as some do, that the kind of consensus we have just been outlining is inimical to a flourishing democracy? How can there be any reservations about the benefits of 'victory' in the 'battle for allegiance' to the 'values of a democratic polity'?

One is inclined to say: If it is the case that the basic political institutions, the basic structural arrangements of a society, the broad objectives or criteria of policy, are supported by the agreement of the great majority, and if these basic arrangements include extensive rights of political participation, organization and dissent, then surely this indicates, so far as it goes, that it is a free and democratic society. If there is a wide and strong consensus supportive of the fundamental democratic values and norms, then it seems a paradox to allege that this consensus can itself be restrictive of democratic activity. We may be inclined to say that those who complain of the restrictive effects of 'consensus politics' are unsuccessful minorities complaining that it is the wrong values, norms or policies that the consensus protects. And no doubt this is sometimes the case. But such a reply evades the more general and important question. What is at issue is the general proposition that too great or high a measure of consensus has a bad effect on the condition of political and social life.

The point from which the argument must begin is that consensus politics in which there is a very wide measure of consensus of the kinds just outlined narrows the range of issues raised in political life, of the alternatives that are able to get considered. This is, of course, true; we have already said that one 'function' of consensus is precisely to narrow the alternatives, limit the spread of issues, that become the subjects of consideration, negotiation and conflict within the political system. And, as we agreed, this is one of the chief ways in which consensus contributes to the stability and continuity of political systems. If we now enquire why this 'function' should also be capable of producing effects inimical to democratic values and activities, we are forced again to reflect upon the nature of consensus. Once more we encounter the fact that consensus is ambiguous in its nature and therefore equivocal in its political and social significance.

As we have argued, for a significant part of any consensus group the compliance constituting the consensus will usually amount to little more than habituation. Some of it will be the expression of inertia, indifference, ignorance, lack of political or social imagination, or absence of a sense of involvement or concern. A consensus partly constituted in these ways can be effectively 'supportive' or 'permissive' (in Key's terms) although clearly it represents an extremely low level of commitment. But, in its general social effects, it can be very repressive. For certain issues the weight of complacency and indifference can effectively inhibit that 'calm and objective appraisal of alternatives' of which Dahl speaks. It is not difficult to provide examples of minorities which may suffer severe injustices and are unable to secure any consideration of their claims because of the consensual indifference of the majority. This is especially the case in systems in which parties compete for power by pursuing 'coalescent strategies' to secure the support of significant interest groups. Parties tend to select issues which promise the greatest electoral advantage and the least electoral risk. The consensus group is not necessarily opposed to the interests or claims of an underprivileged minority; rather, its indifference, and habituation to the *status quo*, create an atmosphere in which it is impossible for certain issues to compel the attention of those who carry on the processes of discussion and policy formation.

That such situations occur provides the most plausible justification—consistent with general democratic values—of some forms of political activity outside the normal processes of public discussion and voting. Passive resistance, occasional resort to more direct uses of force and so on, are sometimes not only a sufficient but a necessary step in forcing a consideration of beliefs, interests or claims ignored by the consensus group. It can be argued that such manifestations as suffragette demonstrations in England early in the century, or the passive and sometimes active resistance and protest by oppressed racial or religious minorities, may have a democratic justification in so far as the prevailing consensus has inhibited consideration through the conventional democratic political channels of serious social interests and issues. It is often notable in such cases how quickly the justice of the claims of dissenting minorities comes to be acknowledged, which suggests that the consensus, although stable and resistant, was not founded on strong commitment. And we can often say in such cases that it is unlikely that without the therapeutic shock of force or 'direct action' the general recognition of the legitimacy of the unconsidered claims would have come about.

We might say that the extent to which a society really is governed by democratic values is related to its readiness to consider the interests and the claims of all its members. Note that to 'consider' does not necessarily mean 'accede to'. Thus, to the extent that 'direct action' outside the formal democratic institutions is sometimes necessary to attract consideration, its effects may be to enhance the democratic quality of a community. This would be one argument employed to defend the 'right to strike', but it can easily be employed in defence of many other varieties of 'direct action'. It is, of course, partly a moral argument: it supports itself partly by referring to the moral narrowness, indifference or inconsiderateness of those who are more or less satisfied with their situation, who will not readily attend to proposals and demands which threaten to disturb habitual and acceptable social arrangements. Thus, when considering the extent to which consensus in support of democratic values and procedures, and the 'coalescent strategies' to which Dahl refers, do make it possible for weight to be given to a wide range of diverse group interests or demands, we must not forget to take into account the effects of the complacency, narrowness and indifference of the relatively satisfied parts of the community.

Of course this argument cannot be used as a *general* justification of 'direct action' or action backed by force. The different forms of 'direct action' are often anti-democratic in their use and effects. They may be so used as to block the operation of the normal or central democratic procedures; for example, demonstrations, force or intimidation may disrupt the conduct of public meetings and elections. Sometimes force reaches a level at which it replaces democratic discussion, free and open elections, and the choice of a representative government. There are no general rules or principles which tell us what kinds or levels of 'direct action' enhance and do not hinder the wider consideration of a variety of viewpoints and claims. Every case has to be judged on its own merits and in its own circumstances. What we can say is that there are circumstances in which action outside the legally or formally recognized processes of parliamentary democratic politics does counteract the frequently constricting effects of political or social consensus, and does open the way to a wider, perhaps more just, consideration of interests and issues that may well be important for some individuals and groups. These might otherwise remain submerged.

Thus, perhaps the main point of critics of 'consensus politics' is the constricting influence of entrenched consensus. This state of affairs is of course accentuated when accompanied by what we may call, very loosely, 'élite consensus': that is, a consensus of the élites and the organizations that have the most say in forming public opinion, in conducting the processes of discussion and publicity, forming policies and controlling the machinery of administration and government. This condition no doubt stabilizes a political system, but it obviously limits the opportunities of citizens to express dissent, or to be brought into contact with a variety of movements of social thinking and aspiration which may suggest alternatives to what is enforced by the prevailing consensus.

The totalitarian states have been the most extreme examples of the control of almost all organizations or associations by a single ruling party, when all associations are required to reflect or subordinate themselves to uniform policies and ideologies. Nothing comparable to totalitarian forms can be found in the pluralistic, 'polyarchal', Western democracies. Nevertheless, 'convergence' in the thinking and policies of the major political parties and the formation of an unusually high level of social consensus do have effects that inhibit and stultify the responsiveness of a system to all the forces active within it. The decline of 'structural oppositions' within some Western democracies during the past quarter of a century or more may well be interpreted as a weakening of rather than a victory for democratic ways of life: in particular, as a narrowing of the range of moral imagination and concern about the economic, social and political organization of the highly industrialized democracies. The decline of opposition which expresses itself through and within central institutions cannot be assumed to demonstrate the total absence of social sentiment, aspiration and ideology at odds with the values and arrangements supported by the dominant consensus.

It would perhaps be fair to say that a great deal of the very recent political science and political philosophy of the Western democracies has been too preoccupied with the analysis of stability as a value and a problem to pay much attention to the positive roles of conflict and dissent. For example, it has been somewhat fashionable among political sociologists to emphasize the positive functions of political apathy. A number of political sociologists have stressed the manner in which a marginal, intermittent, low-keyed popular concern with political issues assists the working of tolerant, coherent, stable democratic politics. No doubt this is true; but it is also true that it is just this complacent apathy which is part of the constitution of that consensus some of the effects of which are restrictive and repressive. Again, praise for the 'end of ideology' may well be a shallow and purblind political philosophy.

For it may be argued that it is impossible for politics ever to be completely non-ideological; at least, impossible for democratic politics ever to be so. Ideologies are made up in part of sets of moral beliefs or attitudes, including moral attitudes concerning the broad and basic structural aspects of a society. In so far as a stable democratic polity requires a significant measure of consensus about 'basic' or 'central' values (as the sociologists of consensus and integration themselves assert), then it requires an ideological consensus; and certainly the consensus that is alleged to characterize the affluent Western democracies is in part an ideological one. If this is so, the truth is not so much that Western democracies have become non-ideological in their politics but rather that ideological *conflict* has become less prominent. And in the absence of ideological divergence and conflict, the consensus-supported ideology is usually latent or unexpressed and unexamined.

Now there are many reasons for believing that the absence of ideological conflict is not a good condition for a society to be in. The politicians of a highly industrialized complex democracy, and the other leaders of great organizations who enter into the processes of negotiation, are bound to concern themselves with adjustment, stability or compromise. The many powerful constraints under which they act (and retain their influence or power) do not allow them normally to concern themselves with the deeper or wider-ranging moral and social dimensions of basic economic, social and political structures. The politics of industrialized democracies is necessarily a politics of adjustment, piecemeal change, coalescent strategies. The deeper questions have to be raised outside of the realm of organized, day-by-day politics. Historically, such issues have usually been raised in ideological, doctrinaire and utopian forms which appear remote from practical politics, and often seem irrational. Nevertheless, although ideologies have seldom deserved to be taken seriously as *policies*, they have often exercised an influence over a long period of time, and have percolated into the thinking of practical politicians, other men of power, and members of the wider society. The radical English democrats of the seventeenth century, the Wildmans and Rainboroughs, the socialist thinkers of the nineteenth century, the Chartists, may have been in their own times (and often for long after) remote from the practicalities and possibilities of real politics; but they represented a stream of social thinking which, given time and favourable conditions, came to impregnate the articulate policies and inarticulate common feeling which influenced the shaping of modern democratic society. It could be argued that the existence and continuous expression of such partly submerged streams of ideology (however irrational they may sometimes seem) is a necessary condition for the moral progress of a society.

The importance of ideological dissensus may also be brought out by invoking arguments similar to some of those used by Mill in his defence of freedom of expression. Mill argued in *Liberty* that even if established beliefs are true, they may become dry and unassimilated husks of truth unless they are forced to hold their own against criticism and dissent. In somewhat the same way the values and concepts of democracy tend to become empty and false. They continue to be professed and they retain, of course, a significant contact with the nature of what actually occurs. Some of their original meaning is, nevertheless, attenuated or obscured as they come to be applied to new forms of political organization and procedure very different from those to which they originally referred. Even some of the twentieth-century dictatorships try to recommend themselves by borrowing some of the language of democracy. In the large industrial democracies of the present age, how attenuated in practice have become such concepts as the 'consent' of the governed, 'majority' rule, 'representative' government, 'responsibility' of the government to the governed, democratic 'participation'. The tendency is for actual organization and practice on the one side and concepts, norms or values on the other to diverge. Or, perhaps more accurately, for the latter—which comprise the democratic ideology—to take on something of the character of ceremonial or ritualistic language: to become less and less descriptive of the true character of actual political processes.

To some extent this is an inevitable process. Ideologies are usually utopian or unrealistic; moral notions and aspirations are compelled to give way before the deflating judgement of political and social inexorabilities. They are constantly, and usually tacitly, being 'redefined' in practice. This process may explain and justify the common view that ideologies are epiphenomenal—causally irrelevant to the real processes of political action and development; or that they are 'false consciousness'. Such views, though they have their share of truth, are one-sided. While it is true that ideological notions are redefined under the pressure of circumstances, it is also true that circumstances are open to ideological judgement. There is a dialectical process: throughout time there is both a shaping and reshaping of ideological concepts by practice and circumstance, and also a shaping of practice by the slow pressure of ideological or moral norms and ideals.

Political philosophers engage in a dual activity: redefining abstract concepts of political or social organization to preserve their relevance to what are judged to be the 'necessities' of social life, and also judging the actual in terms of value-impregnated concepts of social practice and organization. And because empiricism or 'realism' have become such strong imperatives of contemporary social thinking, much recent Western political philosophy and sociology, which has been busy reformulating the 'theory of democracy', has tended to concentrate far more on the first of these operations than on the second.[8]

In the absence of a considerable volume of ideological activity within a society the terms of the so-called 'common value system' naturally become blurred or equivocal. Their meanings become so attenuated in consequence of their being applied so widely to changed situations that they lose much of their original moral point and force. They may function less and less as *norms* that do really order and control political or social practice and more and more as simply conventional formulas of justification and declarations of faith. Of course, within the Western democracies not all of the concepts and norms of democracy have suffered an equal erosion. For example, the norm of free and regular elections is no doubt more strongly maintained than 'government by consent', popular 'participation' or 'equality' in its many different forms. But it would have to be allowed that some of the key concepts of classical democratic ideology now apply only in Pickwickian senses.

Now, one would expect that when norms and values are adhered to with some strength, and are operative in regulating and informing practice, they would be found to occasion some measure of debate and dissent. We mentioned in the last chapter, in discussing the existence or non-existence of consensus about 'basic values', the different interpretations and emphases one can detect in the versions of what democracy is that are current in a Western democratic society. The absence of dissent and conflict about ideologies or basic values, the sort of value consensus that is supposed to have emerged in the Western democracies, may indicate a weakening in the normative or moral force of some of the democratic concepts and ideals. If consensus has really been attained, that may connote only in part victory in the struggle for allegiance to the values of democracy; it may also in part reveal a growth of indifference towards some of the values, a decline in the impetus towards democracy.

For such reasons as these greater ideological consensus, greater integration and stability, are not necessarily to be welcomed. Of course, it is not easy to interpret the significance of the decline of opposition to which the writers we quoted earlier point; one possible interpretation is that modern industrial democracies have achieved a degree of accommodation to the established political and economic structures that makes more difficult the expression of unorthodox beliefs and nonconforming values. And this could be a mark of a weakening of democratic activity; because we might argue that when there is in a society a variety of different ideologies, there are more long-run options before the rank and file of citizens, and the 'choices' available in the long run to the members of a community are wider.

It may be the case that ordinary citizens have more chance of being involved in political activity, or at least of being caught up in political movements, at times when wider ideological issues are raised and freely debated. Much of the current talk about increasing the chances of political 'participation' concentrates on participation in an extremely individualistic sense: the participation by individuals in the decision-making activities of a society or association. Hence the attention paid to voluntary associations by those who believe that there should be more participation by the ordinary citizen; most advocates of a more 'participatory' democracy are individualists and voluntarists.[9] This is an emphasis that needs to be qualified by attention to the nature and role of political and social *movements*: historically speaking, popular participation has in large part been a matter of participating in or being activated by political movements. This has been, and may continue to be, at least as important a form of popular or widespread political participation as the more individualistic and voluntaristic forms usually emphasized by contemporary democrats of a radical stamp.

And we may suggest that movements in which large numbers are either involved, or which communicate to large numbers the experience of serving a cause, of being themselves involved in the active life of the polity, identify themselves by the body of ideological belief and sentiment which they embody. Georges Sorel may have developed his notions of 'the myth of the general strike', 'the ethic of the producer' and the like, in unacceptable forms. But he may nevertheless have seen an important truth: that political action which can involve or affect large numbers will always be ideological politics, that is, politics which involves broad issues and moral concerns. On the other hand, it could well be that the politics of 'incrementalism', of bargaining, negotiation and adjustment, is a form of politics that will almost inevitably accord a central role to political, bureaucratic or organizational élites and thereby tend to exclude the rank and file from the experience of political involvement.

These are matters of high speculation, of course. We raise them here merely to suggest that fashionable views about the superiority

5

of non-ideological politics, and about the positive role of value consensus in providing a solid foundation for a well-ordered democracy, are highly problematical. It is certainly arguable that there are dimensions of democracy not taken into account in these models of a democratic society.

7/A Last Word about Consent

Much earlier it was argued that 'consent' and 'consensus' are not sharply separable concepts. They refer to attitudes and forms of behaviour that can roughly be arranged along a continuum. Much of what makes up those states of agreement and conformity or compliance normally found in a society and described as 'consensus' can be regarded as being a weak or low-level type of consent: weak, that is to say, if contrasted with those stronger senses of 'consent' according to which consent stands for an active or willed, and especially *a priori* permission for, or assent to, what a government does. Since a good deal has now been said about the nature and role of consensus in modern industrial democracies, let us return to the 'status of consent', by which we mean in particular this: To what extent is it true to say that consent of the governed is the criterion by which the legitimacy of democratic governments and their policies is to be judged?

It seems that consent in its *strongest* senses is not a very central characteristic of modern democracies. It is often possible to assert that a government has, at an election, received a mandate for a piece of legislation it proposes, but it is also true that the notion of the mandate itself has but an equivocal place in the orthodox democratic creeds of contemporary democratic states. It is only a small minority (if any at all) who would now contend that governments are not entitled to pass legislation which does not have the backing of a specific mandate. Some theorists take the view that, while it cannot be accepted as a general principle that governments should possess a mandate for everything they do, there are especially important types of legislation (for example, alteration of the constitution or nationalization of an important industry) that a government should never enact unless it has previously announced its intention at a general election. But in prevailing democratic doctrine there is certainly no consensus about the requirement of a mandate. Even the questions of what in fact constitutes a mandate, or how one decides whether a government has a mandate or not for some particular measure, occasion serious difficulties of their own. And no one will deny that the vast mass of what a modern government enacts has not in any sense received the prior approval or consent of the electorate; probably there is no one who would claim that government would be possible if this requirement were imposed.

We can, of course, reconcile these facts with the concept of consent if we are willing to attenuate the meaning of consent. We may say that the policies and acts of a government enjoy the consent of (the majority of) the governed because what it has done has aroused no significant opposition or criticism. We can say that because of the understandings that now obviously control the working of political machinery, the majority that has elected a government has expressed in advance its consent to (its acceptance of the legitimacy of) whatever the government decides to do. But clearly these are rather weak senses of consent; and it is very doubtful, also, whether these assertions do accurately describe the situations and attitudes present in the democratic community.

When we consider prevailing doctrine and attitudes with regard to the claims of consent of the governed, we must conclude that there is no agreed coherent doctrine. Some men would certainly deny (if not as a general proposition at least from time to time with reference to particular cases) that, in voting for a party that forms a government, they have accepted in advance the legitimacy of whatever the government chooses to do. This may tempt us to say, then, that there are tacit understandings about what a government will not do, about the limits and constraints it will observe in its exercise of power, and that governments may claim to have the consent of the governed in so far as they observe these understandings. No doubt, we may say, a government will do many things with which a minority or majority of citizens will disagree; but the government has the consent of the governed to the extent that it respects certain expectations and unexpressed understandings concerning things it will not do. This is related to 'agreement about fundamentals', which doubtless does point to an important feature of consent as it is present in modern parliamentary democracies. But it does not take us very far: it refers again to one of the weaker senses of consent (this state of affairs would nowadays be more likely to be described as consensus). It also provokes practical difficulties: it is unlikely that all members of the community have the same expectations or understandings concerning the limits of action that a government will observe. In countries such as Britain and Australia, Labour governments no doubt meet many of the expectations of the business and industrial communities; it is not certain that they endear themselves to many of their trade-union supporters by so doing.

There is also a very strong strain in prevailing democratic assumption according to which it is not expected that the policies or actions of a government should be supported by the prior (or even contemporaneous) consent of the governed. There is the assumption that it is the duty of a government to govern: to make decisions and develop policies as changing situations demand, and to supply leadership. Governments are apt to be condemned if they fall short in the matter of day-to-day leadership and decision making, or if they appear to be too much influenced by popular clamour or pressure.

In short, it is very apparent that when we consider the actual political criteria, norms and values causally at work within the political system and which affect practice, there are competing strains. On the whole the democratic assumption that puts a relatively heavy emphasis on the consent of the governed has had to give way to opposing strains. It is interesting that those versions which have given a central role to consent in its stronger forms— for example, doctrines about referendum, initiative and recall— have been treated in most Western democracies as democratic heresies. Equally, ideas about the desirability of widespread and continuous popular participation in political activity, including decision making, have been submerged (although not entirely powerless) elements in the ideology or compound of ideologies that have actually prevailed in the practice of the democracies. And also ideas about industrial democracy or about worker participation in the control of industry, although they had wide currency in Britain in the early years of this century and have also been much discussed in some European countries, have not greatly influenced democratic practice; they have been overshadowed by other notions of what democracy is and requires.[1] It is possible that some of these submerged strains of thought may enjoy a revival although there is little to indicate its immediate likelihood. But that such diverse strains of democratic ideology are present within an industrial democracy, and that they reach some sort of accommodation with one another in the actual practice of government and administration, is another reason for suspecting that the appearance of consensus that emerges from time to time may not quite accurately reflect the state of feeling and attitude within the democratic society.

At all events, we may say in general that the mainstream of democratic thought and practice does seem to have rejected ideas of continuous popular consent and control, and has emphasized instead a different doctrine. This is the doctrine that a popularly elected government ought to enjoy and to employ the authority to make its own decisions. There has not only been a tendency for authority to become more concentrated but also a tendency at the level of ideology or assumption for this trend to be supported. But the doctrine as just stated is surrounded by a variety of qualifications, some of them precise enough (and sufficiently supported by consensus) to be applied as norms, others more equivocal and vague. One of the firmer qualifications is that governments should, in regularly held elections, test *post factum* the presence or absence of consent. Another is that opportunities must be provided for consent and dissent to manifest themselves continuously and perpetually in open discussion.

It seems clear that both in actual practice and in the assumptions and expectations of ruling democratic doctrine in large, industrialized Western democracies the norm that legitimate government requires the consent of the governed is maintained only in the *weaker* senses of consent. Of course, the nature of political, economic and social change has supported this ideological trend. The developments in question have been spelt out *ad nauseam*: there is no reason here to say anything more about problems of size, or how the greater volume, complexity and technicality of most of the questions with which modern governments deal have been unfavourable to the survival of notions of consent in its more literal, demanding senses. It is even true to say that the greater 'openness' of modern democracies, that is, their capacity to allow an ever-wider range of social groups and organizations to make demands and exert pressures on governments, has also served to strengthen governmental authority. This has made still more plausible the idea that strong and centralized authority is necessary for affecting and maintaining those adjustments of a mass of competing interests which are nowadays commonly taken to be the main function and output of government.

Government by the consent of the governed is, therefore, a principle that has had to contend with extremely unsympathetic political and social realities. But it is worth asking in what senses it may still be said to be operative as a constitutive idea in the practice of modern democratic states, and in what senses it is still clearly defensible.

We can say that consent of the governed, in so far as that can be elicited through free and open elections, is still, and can still be, maintained as a criterion of a democratic regime. True, the more closely elections are studied and understood, the more difficult it may be to say what sort of consent exactly (or consent to what exactly and by whom) is expressed in the electorate's verdict. Further, as we noted in commenting on the status of the 'mandate' concept, men disagree as regards the nature of the consent a governing party should be expected to secure. All in all, democratic elections are a very ambiguous, imperfect means of eliciting consent, or of registering its presence or absence.

Nevertheless it can reasonably be maintained that when the members of a community can make a decision as to which of a number of competing parties and sets of political leaders they prefer to govern them, this increases the probability that the government will enjoy a wider range of consent, of a higher order, than one would expect to be the case in political regimes where governments are not exposed to popular judgement and rejection.

The point is made in this guarded way because it is perfectly conceivable that an absolute prince or even a modern highly authoritarian government may rule with the strong consent of most of their subjects: men sometimes love their chains. Perhaps the most we can say, then, is that it is probable that, over the long run, there will be a wider and a stronger body of consent under freely and regularly elected governments than in other types of regime. It is to be noted that we talk in terms of amounts and levels of consent. 'Government by the consent of the governed' is too broad and loose a phrase to apply to communities ruled by elected governments; there are always some who do not consent but are opposed and dissident. And as we have argued, a specification of the meaning of consent that would embrace all of the governed within the usual system of representative democracy would leave the criterion of government with the consent of the governed without a cutting edge.

With these, and doubtless other, qualifications we can say then that free elections are a useful means of reducing the level of dissent, and of increasing the level of accord between governed and government. This would be a statement of the minimum function so far as consent is concerned. Elections may do more than this of course. On those occasions on which specific policies are submitted by a party in the course of an election, and clearly endorsed by the majority of electors, we achieve consent in its strongest sense: permission or endorsement prior to the event. But elections are very complex processes; it is impossible to claim that everything that transpires or is done in the election of a government connotes consent of this order.

It would be common ground among the supporters of Western-style democracy that free, continuous discussion also extends the range and raises the level of consent. Probably most people would also support a stronger proposition: that free discussion is a necessary condition for a high level of consent. Only where there is free discussion, the standard argument runs, are the consent and dissent of a community being continuously expressed; and only so are governments continuously acted upon, and made responsive to, popular judgement and demand.

There are very obvious restrictions on the power of open discussion to serve these ends. Effective discussion requires publicity: only when the activities of governments are widely known, the information relevant to its decisions widely available, the issues before it (or not before it) generally understood, can public opinion or public demand accomplish the tasks often attributed to them in the more simplified accounts of democracy. And free discussion and publicity (which often has to be achieved in the teeth of governments and others who have an interest in silence or secrecy) require leaders of opinion, organizations, and organs of expression which raise issues, disseminate information, and generally help to promote and sustain argument. The extent to which free discussion will operate as a consent-producing process will depend, among other things, on the extent to which such conditions as these are fulfilled.

There are circumstances in contemporary democracies which place limits upon their achievement. In spite of the enormous growth of publicity and the mass media, it is not easy to create adequate publicity concerning the problems, thinking and decisions of governments. Governments often shun publicity about their own plans, not only in matters of foreign policy but in other areas of policy as well. They very often claim that it is not in the public interest that the public should be kept informed about policies that are being evolved, decisions that are being prepared. The servants of the state tend to set a high value on what some would call 'discretion' and others 'the cult of secrecy'. Indeed, publicity is one of the ambiguous or problematic areas of modern democracies: everyone will agree that the processes of democracy in some sense require a great deal of publicity; on the other hand not only governments but most other great social organizations cannot but feel that their work is not always best performed in the full public gaze.

So far as governments are concerned, there are some solid reasons for being distrustful of too much publicity. Continuous public clamour and a multitude of continuous pressures do not necessarily provide a favourable atmosphere in which solutions can be worked out and decisions taken. Incessant publicity and public debate can confuse and obstruct coherent and disinterested governmental thinking. Much policy making and administration depend upon the gaining of information, upon exchanges of views with other organizations, where confidentiality is a condition of the whole process. And apart from considerations of this order, there are the difficulties of communicating adequately and accurately the often highly complicated and highly technical data and theories upon which policy decisions are made. It would seem plausible to assume that in what some recent American writers have been calling 'the knowledgeable society'—the society in which social decision and action are increasingly based upon complicated bodies of information and upon social and other scientific theories—the gap of incomprehension between decision makers and administrators (in all large organizations) on the one side, and the general or lay public on the other, will be increasingly hard to bridge.

If it is true, then, that it is a desideratum that, as much as possible, government should enjoy the consent of the governed, and if it is also true that free discussion and abundant information and publicity are important means of heightening the level of consent, problems connected with publicity will be increasingly central problems for democratic theory and practice. Not only practical questions about how information can be disseminated but also questions as to how much or what sorts of publicity ought to be available and on what occasions. What sorts of publicity does the public interest justify and require—not only so far as the activities of governments are concerned but also other organizations which affect the public interest such as universities or professional associations? As we suggested, in this area of democratic thinking and practice there are opposing norms or criteria at work: it is certainly not universally acknowledged that prior or concurrent assent to governmental decisions is the supreme or exclusive criterion to be applied, or that, therefore, governments should be expected to do their thinking aloud and in public.

As in the case of free elections we cannot generalize about the efficacy of discussion in raising the level of consent. On particular occasions it can be very efficacious; it happens not infrequently that governments are induced to act, or to refrain from intended action, by the force of public opinion. But such clear cases are, perhaps, exceptional. There are other cases in which it can be said that a government has had the prior consent of the governed. But mostly the consent of the governed, when it does exist, is consent of the weaker forms, expressed after the event, created by the action that it comes to support; and weaker forms yet such as acquiescence, indifference, and the silence that is taken to be consent.

There has always existed one strain of democratic thinking according to which a high level of consent is brought about by widespread, active, popular participation in political affairs, or, more widely, in the conduct of public business. Some still argue that modern democracies do not attain the levels of consent required by the norm of 'government by the consent of the governed' because so few actually participate in the conduct of public affairs except by the relatively insignificant act of periodically voting. And some of those who hold that widespread political participation is a necessary condition of democracy, and of conformity to the norm of government by consent, conclude that membership of voluntary or special associations, and the exercise by such associations of an important role in the political affairs of the community, are therefore vital features of a democratic and consenting society. Smaller, special, voluntary associations are social units within which it is possible for ordinary citizens to enjoy the experience of participation and the exercise of responsibility; and, if these special associations themselves are allowed to perform significant functions in the organization of public affairs, and in the conduct of national government, they also serve as channels connecting the rank and file with the higher organs of government. This is a conception of democratic organization that has been prominent for a long time; in the present century this emphasis on the democratic role of the special association and the social group was characteristic of the earlier forms of political pluralism represented by the guild socialist and the pluralists of the earlier Laskian kind. Among the latter-day pluralists, represented by many contemporary political sociologists, the emphasis is rather different: rather on the organized group or association as 'pressure group', i.e., as a source of pressure on central government within a system of 'polyarchal democracy', not so much on the association as an arena within which citizens experience participation and self-government.

This is a plausible, appealing model of a democratic society. Yet the claim that a high level of consent requires a high level of popular participation, and that therefore 'government by consent' is to be sought by raising the level of participation, has its difficulties. We need not dwell on the practical or institutional difficulties: how can a vast industrial society in fact involve a significant proportion of the community in the processes of discussion, decision making or administration? In this connection the great special associations or organizations have not played quite the role in modern democracies some have demanded of them. Some of them, of course, have come to play extremely important roles; and with the growth of industrial society the organization of particular interests and sections of the community has grown rapidly. But most of those that are politically important have not been conspicuously successful as organs of 'participatory' democracy; they have rather operated as pressure groups protecting the interests of the groups they 'represent'—usually a large part of the members of those groups are not active members of the organizations that represent them. On balance it cannot be said that they have been remarkably effective in extending the practice of popular democracy.

There are other difficulties apart from the practical ones. Would a society which did achieve wider and more continuous participation in fact secure a higher level of consent? Not necessarily. It might provide conditions in which 'veto groups', conflicting opinions and interests of all sorts would be better able to resist one another, to establish a pattern of checks and balances which might produce frustration and dissidence rather than a higher level of consent. Smaller associations than the state often cannot produce any high level of satisfaction for their members because they cannot find a sufficient area of consensus. On a much larger scale, there have been Western democracies, such as France and Weimar

Germany, in which the fragmentation of social interests and political organization have led to great political instability and much political dissidence. We cannot assume that the more participation the higher the level of consent: participation in the common political affairs of a community may be a value in its own right, but it is not necessarily a sufficient condition of securing consent.

We may also ask whether widespread political participation naturally comports with other central structural features of modern industrial democracies. In these democracies, how strong in fact is the *demand* for participation and the forms of direct democracy? What is the historical evidence that greater participation would be sustained by the interests and attitudes of a large part of the community; that it is highly congruent with the modes of life and aspirations of the majority of citizens? We cannot speak as if nonparticipation were a somehow curable sickness of modern democracies; it may be something deeply embedded in the wider structures of such societies.

We have mentioned the now fashionable view that a certain measure of apathy on the part of the majority of the community is a condition that favours liberal democracy. We suggested that it is both favourable to and restrictive of democracy. By and large that has been the condition of the majority of Western democracies, at least for long stretches of time, and those who believe greater participation would enhance democracy and widen consent cannot avoid the question of why, on the whole, popular political interest and participation have existed on such low levels.

There are many characteristics of modern industrial democracies which would appear to account for the normally low level of concern and activity (many of them have been referred to in the course of this book), but there is one in particular that we wish to touch on here.

It is the extremely pluralistic structure of modern industrial societies: their pluralism of interests, activities and ways of life. Not only do circumstances make it enormously difficult for most men to concern themselves with more than a very few of the issues of national politics, but the great majority of people are inevitably absorbed in those particular interests and activities which are, in fact, the substance of their lives. It is through their pursuit of these more special interests (which may be 'private' but may also be social activities of great importance) that most men find their chief fulfilment. It is a mistake to assume that *political* participation is necessarily a 'higher' or morally better form of participation than any other, or that there is something morally defective in a society in which there is not incessant and almost universal interest in political affairs. Of course, absorption in particular or specialized interests does not preclude activity in wider political affairs, and a democratic system of government obviously requires that a large part of the community will interest itself, more or less strongly and continuously, with political questions. But it is not realistic to expect that a very large proportion of citizens will pay more than intermittent and somewhat remote attention to political questions.

These are a few of the reasons why the notion that the way to raise the level of consent is to get more citizens participating more continuously in public affairs is perhaps not plausible. Possibly reconstructing the political and other institutions of industrial democracies would provide better institutional means of common participation. Perhaps it is surprising that there has been so little interest during the present century in the possibilities of institutional reform and innovation to allow more citizens to engage in the government of the state and of lesser communities and associations. There seems to have been very little public interest in the democracies in the structures of basic political institutions for a long time. This may suggest some form of consensus supporting the established constitutional or institutional arrangements; but it also suggests that public interest has turned from questions about political organization to questions about other social objectives— for example, technological and economic growth. It seems that some of the difficulties that face the idea of a more effective 'participatory democracy' lie deeper than the level of political institutional arrangements. They are connected, we suggest, with the logic of the pluralism of modern industrial societies, with the general fact that the role of politics and government cannot be treated as being quite so central in the complex total affairs of modern democratic states as the exponents of democracy as direct participation tend to assume.

Clearly, then, the principle that government should rule with the consent of the governed is scarcely an absolute principle; clearly the concept or requirement of consent enters democratic theory and practice in very complex, even confused ways. That citizens ought to have the opportunity to decide at regular, free elections whether they prefer a particular government or an alternative no one who accepts consent as one criterion of legitimate government is likely to deny. But though this is generally accepted it is not easy to determine (as we have seen) in what ways exactly these standard democratic procedures are believed or expected to satisfy the requirement of consent of the governed.

We have noted that there are very strong reasons against taking consent of the governed as an absolute requirement for the legitimacy of government. This is especially true when consent is being understood in its stronger senses. Against the requirement of popular consent we have to recognize that it is a function and duty of governments to provide political leadership, to perform an initiating role. To apply the stronger senses of consent, and to argue that actions of government have no authority unless endorsed by the consent of citizens (or a majority of them) implies that citizens are capable of greater initiative than can in fact be possible. It is a function of political leaders and governments to identify problems and issues and to propose solutions (not their function alone, of course). They must also attempt to generate consent, partly by argument and explanation, partly by developing policies and courses of action that a large part of the community will approve. This is part of what political authority means: the capacity to lead in ways that in turn establish and sustain the authority of the leaders.

This means that consent, to the extent that it is aroused, must frequently manifest itself during and after the event; that is, while a course of action is being put into effect, or in a later popular judgement, perhaps at an election, when the nature and effects of policies have been seen. In short, governments by their actions mobilize and maintain support; and, this being the case, consent in the form of what we have called (following V. O. Key) 'supportive consensus' will be one of the quite central or fundamental forms of consent within a democracy which apeals to the principle of government by consent.

That is one basic type of governmental process. Another is slightly different: the case where governments must use their own initiative in discovering and developing solutions or policies, but within limits set by very general patterns of social demand or by existing forms of consensus. This is also a constant and basic mode of governmental action. Governments are expected, for example, to find policies that maintain continuing general prosperity; or reduce unemployment; or restore law and order or quieten industrial unrest; or solve an alarming international development. How to do it is their responsibility, but they will be judged eventually by their success. Until then they will be supported if they are visibly attentive to the problems.

We may say that this type of situation involves what has been called 'permissive consensus', and that this again is a form of consent basic or central to any regime based on the consent of the governed.

There is still another type of situation. There are often issues which have aroused very great public interest, issues with respect to which strong and divergent public beliefs and attitudes may exist independently of anything that a government has said or done. For instance, in most countries there are well-entrenched opinions relating to long-standing policies (such as tariff policies or policies concerning control of immigrants); or again relating to long-standing economic or social arrangements such as the distribution of poverty, the ownership and control of an industry, or the hours of opening of the pubs. These are issues concerning which bodies of public opinion exist, and it cannot be said that a government which proposed to change the existing arrangements or policies is supported by a 'permissive consensus'. It might be argued in such cases that the doctrine of consent requires a government, before it acts, to appeal for prior assent to its proposal.

And this claim is frequently conceded in practice: parties competing for office present what they consider their most important proposals. Even so, this is a difficult area where it is impossible to prescribe firm principles; the clear cases shade off into others where the circumstances are much more confused and obscure. Moreover, almost any governmental action which may mobilize consent will also, by disturbing existing interests, generate new sources of dissent. It is impossible in many instances to create a balance of consent and dissent; or, in view of the duty of governments to exercise independent authority, to prescribe principles concerning such a balance that must exist before a government may act.

Obviously when questions of consent are brought down to this level the discussion becomes entirely unreal. There are certain issues with regard to which we can firmly say that governments ought to be assured of prior majority consent before they are entitled to act. (In accordance with this principle, a number of countries with written constitutions require especially severe conditions to be met in the case of constitutional amendments.) But there is also a very wide area within which governments must be expected to assume responsibility and make decisions; in doing so, they act at their peril (granted conditions of regular free elections, freedom of organization and expression of opinion), and the proof of the pudding is in the eating—it remains to be seen whether they have mobilized sufficient consent.

This statement of the status of consent, of course, would not satisfy many who would demand institutional arrangements which make possible more direct and continuous expressions of consent and dissent. We have touched very briefly on these demands and suggested a few reasons why it seems that this is a reading of the principle of government by consent that is unlikely to prove particularly effective in informing or regulating the actual practice of modern democratic government. But those who do take that kind of view differ from others, perhaps, because they attach greater weight to consent as one of the criteria by which governments are appraised, and not only that but to consent in its stronger forms. As against that ranking of the importance of the criterion of consent, we may recognize that governments themselves must make their own judgements concerning the balance between consent and dissent they are willing to live with; and we may argue that, subject to the important qualifications we have set down, the end of government is not exclusively to *maximize consent*. Policies which would produce a greater volume of consent than any alternatives may be subject to serious moral objections on other grounds (the provision of bread and circuses, for example, has never been generally accepted as a very admirable strategy of government); and conversely, policies directed towards morally worthy ends such as alleviation of poverty, reduction of inequality, the countering of racial hatred and discrimination and so on, may, in the particular circumstances prevailing within a society at a given time, be the very reverse of consent-maximizing policies. Thus, consent of the governed is one among a number of values and criteria applicable in judging the legitimacy of a government's authority and of the wisdom and nobility of its policies. People will differ about the relative weights they ascribe to each of these values; there are no general principles which can tell us what is the proper weighting.

Notes
and
References

1/The Problem of Consent

1 The best short study of the history of the doctrine of the social contract from its origins in early Greek thought down to recent times is J. W. Gough, *The Social Contract* (Oxford 1967).
2 I. C. H. McIlwain, *The Growth of Political Thought in the West* (New York 1955), pp. 73-4.
3 G. H. Sabine, *A History of Political Theory* (London 1944), p. 319.
4 J. W. Gough, op. cit., p. 19.
5 Ibid., p. 25.
6 See R. W. and A. J. Carlyle, *A History of Mediaeval Political Theory in the West* (London, 3rd edn, 1930) especially vol. I, part IV, chs. XIX and XX, vol. II, part I, ch. VII.
7 *Defensor Pacis*, quoted in Sabine, *A History of Political Theory*, p. 296.
8 *De concordantia catholica*, II, xiv, quoted in Sabine, p. 319.
9 *The Laws of Ecclesiastical Polity*, in *The works of Mr Richard Hooker in eight books* . . . 3 vols, London 1821. Book I, Section x, Vol. I, p. 156.
10 Ibid., p. 159.
11 Ibid., p. 159.
12 Ibid., p. 158
13 Book VIII, Vol. 3, p. 242.
14 *Second Treatise of Civil Government*, Ch. VIII, Sec. 119.

2/The Meaning of Consent

1 B. Crick, "Freedom as Politics", in P. Laslett and W. G. Runciman (eds), *Philosophy, Politics and Society* (third series, Oxford 1967), p. 203.
2 This is the view of the meaning of consent that Plamenatz took in the original text of *Consent, Freedom and Political Obligation*, first published in 1938. However, in the postscript added to the new paperback edition of 1968, Plamenatz says that he there defined consent too narrowly, and he offers the following account: '. . . it is always to do or to take part in doing something which the doer knows, or is presumed to know, creates in another a right he would not otherwise have'. This is to withdraw from the meaning of the concept as a necessary element 'the granting of a permission or . . . the expression of a wish'. And, in accordance with his new definition, Plamenatz goes on to suggest that 'where there is an established process of election to an office, then, *provided the election is free*, anyone who takes part in the process consents to the authority of whoever is elected to the office'. (p. 170).
3 Cf. Cassinelli, *The Politics of Freedom* (Seattle 1961), 'Consent implies voluntariness and the association of almost every citizen with the government which controls him is clearly involuntary.' (p. 91).
4 Joseph Schumpeter's criticism of "The Classical Theory of Democracy", in his *Capitalism, Socialism and Democracy*, is a detailed development of some of the reasons alluded to in the text.

5 A. Gewirth, "Political Justice", in R. B. Brandt (ed.), *Social Justice* (Prentice-Hall, 1962): 'Government by consent means, rather, that the specific holders of political authority are not independent variables so far as their authority is concerned but are dependent on the votes of the electorate. This entails that the government, as a matter of constitutional requirement, is regularly subjected to a process which passes judgment on it and may transfer its authority to other hands.' (p. 137).

6 'In Britain, at least, there is simply no consensus about the relationship between popular support and claim to political authority. There are two aspects to this relationship. First, there is the question whether a government which has become generally and manifestly unpopular should resign . . . Secondly, how far should a government try to promote particular policies which—as the [public opinion] polls make all too clear—are widely opposed?' (William Plowden in *The Listener*, September 5, 1968.)

3/The Anatomy of Consent

1 See, for example, the discussion by Gewirth in "Political Justice" (R. B. Brandt, *Social Justice*, pp. 131–6).

2 C. J. Friedrich, *A New Belief in the Common Man* (Boston 1942), p. 153ff.

3 One well-known study of this kind is J. W. Prothro and C. W. Grigg, "Fundamental Principles of Democracy: Bases of Agreement and Disagreement", in *Journal of Politics*, Vol. 22, May 1960.

4 R. K. Merton, "Manifest and Latent Functions", in *Social Theory and Social Structure* (Glencoe, Free Press), 1957.

5 "Political Justice", in Brandt, *Social Justice*, pp. 131, 137, 138.

6 R. A. Dahl, *Preface to Democratic Theory* (Chicago 1956).

7 C. E. Lindblom in his *The Intelligence of Democracy* (New York 1965) discusses the manner in which inequalities are accepted as a price for consent; for example, inequalities of power, of representation in parliamentary bodies and so on.

8 In his monograph *A Theory of Stable Democracy* (Princeton 1961), Professor H. Eckstein discusses in a different sense the importance of 'congruence' between government structure and practice and structure and practice in other areas of social organization in accounting for the stability and instability of democratic systems.

9 For example, J. Blondel, *Voters, Parties and Leaders* (Harmondsworth 1966), pp. 81–4.

10 Shils has developed this view in a number of places; for example, in *The Torment of Secrecy* (Glencoe, Ill. 1956).

11 On this, see A. Shonfield, *Modern Capitalism* (London 1965).

12 For a general discussion of associations and organizations in the context of the notion of government by consent, see C. Frankel, *The Democratic Prospect* (New York 1962), chapter IV, "Recovering Government by Consent".

4/Theories of Consensus

1 V. O. Key, *Public Opinion and American Democracy* (New York 1961). p. 27 and p. 584 ff.

2 *Cours de Philosophie Positive*, Book VI, Ch. III.

3 I. L. Horowitz, "Consensus, Conflict and Cooperation: A Sociological Inventory", in *Social Forces*, 41 (December 1962).

4 London, 1968, pp. 138–45, 160–72.

5 For an interesting brief discussion of the relation between Comte and Durkheim on the subject of consensus, see A. W. Gouldner's introduction to Durkheim's *Socialism* (New York 1962).

6 The following passage is an unusually uncompromising statement of the 'conflict model': 'There is a third notion which, together with change and conflict, constitutes the instrumentarium of the conflict model of society: the notion of constraint. From the point of view of this model, societies and social organisations are held together not by consensus but by constraint, not by universal agreement but by the coercion of some by others. It may be useful for some purposes to speak of the "value system" of a society, but in the conflict model, such characteristic values are ruling rather than common, enforced rather than accepted, at any given point of time. And, as conflict generates change, so constraint may be thought of as generating conflict.' Ralf Dahrendorf, "Out of Utopia", *American Journal of Sociology*, 64, September 1958. In his *Class and Class Conflict in Contemporary Society* (London 1959), Dahrendorf deals with this opposition in a much more cautious and eclectic manner.

7 The following formulation itself expresses a consensus of contemporary pluralistic political theorists: 'Prior to politics, beneath it, enveloping it, restricting it, conditioning it, is the underlying consensus on policy that usually exists in the society among the predominant portion of the politically active members.' R. A. Dahl, *Preface to Democratic Theory* (Chicago 1956), pp. 132–3.

8 C. Wright Mills, *The Power Elite* (New York 1956); Talcott Parsons, "On the Concept of Political Power", in his *Sociological Theory and Modern Society* (New York 1967). Parsons directly attacks Mills' view in his review article on *The Power Elite* in *World Politics*, Vol. 10, October 1957.

9 T. Parsons, *Sociological Theory and Modern Society*, p. 6.

10 T. Parsons, *The Structure of Social Action* (New York 1937), pp. 389, 392, 395.

11 R. C. Angell, *Free Society and Moral Crisis* (Ann Arbor 1965), p. 40.

12 G. Myrdal, *An American Dilemma* (New York 1944). The discussion of 'valuations' and their mode of operation in society is still an important contribution to the subject we are touching on here. These and other writings by Myrdal on the subject are brought together in his *Value in Social Theory* (London 1957), especially pp. 65–88.

13 R. Dahrendorf, *Class and Class Conflict in Industrial Society* (London 1959), pp. 161, 162.

14 Writings by Shils relevant to the theory of consensus include *The Torment of Secrecy* (Glencoe 1956); his article on "Centre and Periphery", in *The Logic of Personal Knowledge: Essays Presented to Michael Polanyi* (London 1961) and the article on "Consensus", in the *International Encyclopedia of the Social Sciences* (New York 1968).

15 T. Parsons in E. Burdick and A. J. Brodbeck, *American Voting Behavior* (New York 1959). Parsons' chapter, " 'Voting' and the Equilibrium of the American Political System" is reprinted in his *Sociological Theory and Modern Society*.

16 C. J. Friedrich, *Man and His Government* (New York 1963), p. 238.

17 H. Eckstein, *A Theory of Stable Democracy* (Princeton 1961), p. 31.

18 E. Haas, *Beyond the Nation State* (Stanford 1964), p. 39.

19 V. O. Key, *Public Opinion and American Democracy* (New York 1961), p. 32.

5/Consensus and Democracy

1 H. J. McClosky, "Consensus and Ideology in American Politics", *American Political Science Review*, June 1964.

2 F. R. Leavis (ed.), *Mill on Bentham and Coleridge* (London 1950), p. 123.

3 Quoted by C. J. Friedrich, *A New Image of the Common Man* (Boston 1950), p. 156.

4   See, for example, S. M. Lipset, *Political Man* (London 1960); R. E. Lane, "The Politics of Consensus in an Age of Affluence", *American Political Science Review*, December 1965.

5   There is a brief and lucid sketch of such a model (presented in the form of a criticism of Parsons' general theories) in D. Lockwood, "Some Comments on 'The Social System' ", *British Journal of Sociology*, Vol. 7, No. 2, 1956.

6   G. Almond and S. Verba, *The Civic Culture* (Princeton 1963).

7   One of the best discussions of resemblances and differences between democracies with respect to some of the questions concerning us here is R. A. Dahl (ed.), *Political Oppositions in Western Democracies* (New Haven 1966).

6/Consensus, Dissent and Ideology

1   Ernest Gellner in his article, "Democracy and Industrialisation" (*Archives Europeennes de Sociologie*, VIII, 1967) brings out clearly the resemblance between the Leninist critique of 'bourgeois democracy' and the views of Western political scientists who emphasize consensus as a necessary condition of parliamentary democracy. (Friedrich, as we noted, had already seen the affiliation.) But when Gellner says that 'what the modern consensus theory has done is simply to transform the reproach into a merit', this is a bit too simple because it ignores the complexity of that 'modern consensus theory'.

2   As typical of many of the assertions about the modern consensus that could be quoted from the works of political scientists we may cite the following passage from Lipset's *Political Man*: '. . . the fundamental political problems of the industrial revolution have been solved: the workers have achieved industrial and political citizenship; the conservatives have accepted the welfare state; and the democratic left has recognised that an increase in overall state power carries with it more dangers to freedom than solutions for economic problems'. (p. 406).

3   E. Shils, "Centre and Periphery", in *The Logic of Personal Knowledge; Essays Presented to Michael Polanyi on His 70th Birthday* (London 1961).

4   One of the most thorough expositions of this concept of political activity will be found in R. A. Dahl and C. E. Lindblom, *Politics, Economics and Welfare* (New York 1953).

5   R. A. Dahl (ed.), *Political Opposition in Western Democracies* (New Haven 1966), p. 395.

6   Ibid., p. 398.

7   For discussions of these issues by a writer who puts great weight on the role of consensus with regard to the stability of democracies, see Lucian Pye, *Aspects of Political Development* (Boston 1966).

8   I have discussed this 'dual activity' more fully in an article, "Political Philosophy and Political Sociology", *Australian and New Zealand Journal of Sociology*, Vol. 1, No. 1, April 1965.

9   See the discussion of the role of voluntary associations by Charles Frankel in the chapter "Recovering Government by Consent" in his *The Democratic Prospect* (New York 1962).

7/A Last Word About Consent

1   See the discussion in H. A. Clegg's *Industrial Democracy and Nationalisation* (Oxford 1951) of the opposition between 'direct democracy' and 'pressure group democracy' as applied to industrial management. A very recent discussion of 'industrial democracy' in Norway, Yugoslavia, West Germany and Britain will be found in F. E. Emery and Einar Thorsrud, *Form and Content in Industrial Democracy* (London 1969).

Bibliography

Select Bibliography

CASSINELLI, C., *The Politics of Freedom: An Analysis of the Modern Democratic State*, University of Washington Press, Seattle 1961.

DAHRENDORF, R., "Out of Utopia", *American Journal of Sociology*, Vol. 64, September 1958.

GEWIRTH, A., "Political Justice", R. B. Brandt (ed.), *Political Justice*, Prentice Hall, Englewood Cliffs, N.J. 1962. A Spectrum Book.

HOROWITZ, I. L., "Consensus, Conflict and Cooperation: A Sociological Inventory", *Social Forces*, Vol. 41, December 1962.

LANE, R. E., "The Politics of Consensus in an Age of Affluence", *American Political Science Review*, Vol. 59, December 1965.

LIPSITZ, LEWIS, "The Study of Consensus", *International Encyclopedia of the Social Sciences*, Macmillan Company and Free Press, N.Y. 1968.

LOCKE, J., *Two Treatises of Civil Government*, J. M. Dent, London 1949. Everyman's Library No. 751.

McCLOSKY, H. S., "Consensus and Ideology in American Politics", *American Political Science Review*, Vol. 58, 1964.

PITKIN, HANNA, "Obligation and Consent", *American Political Science Review*, Vol. 59, December 1965 and Vol. 60, March 1966.

PLAMENATZ, J. P., *Consent, Freedom and Political Obligation*, 2nd edn, Oxford University Press, London 1968.

SHILS, E. A., "Consensus", *International Encyclopedia of the Social Sciences*, Macmillan Company and Free Press, New York 1968.

General Bibliography

ALMOND, G. A. and VERBA, S., *The Civic Culture: Political Attitudes and Democracy in Five Nations*, Princeton University Press, Princeton, N.J. 1963; Oxford University Press, London 1964.

ANGELL, R. C., *Free Society and Moral Crisis*, University of Michigan Press, Ann Arbor 1958.

ARISTOTLE, *The Politics*, translated with an introduction, notes and appendix by E. Barker, Clarendon Press, Oxford 1946.

BACHRACH, P., "Elite Consensus and Democracy", *Journal of Politics*, Vol. 24, 1962.

BAILEY, F. G., *Strategems and Spoils: A Social Anthropology of Politics*, Explorations in Anthropology Series, Schocken, New York 1969; Basic Books, Blackwell, Oxford 1969.

BARKER, E., *Greek Political Theory: Plato and his Predecessors*, 3rd edn, Methuen, London 1947.

BENDIX, R. and LIPSET, S. M., "Political Sociology", *Current Sociology*, Vol. 6, 1957.

BLONDEL, JEAN, *Voters, Parties and Leaders: The Social Fabric of British Politics*, Penguin Books, Harmondsworth, Middlesex 1963.

BOSANQUET, B., *The Philosophical Theory of the State*, 4th edn, Macmillan, London 1951.

CARLYLE, SIR R. W. and CARLYLE, A. J. (joint author), *A History of Mediaevla Political Theory in the West*, Blackwood, London 1950, 6 vols.

CHRISTOPH, J. B., "Consensus and Cleavage in British Political Ideology", *American Political Science Review*, Vol. 59, September 1965.

CICERO, *De Re Publica. On the Commonwealth*, translated, with an introduction by G. H. Sabine and S. B. Smith, Bobbs Merrill, Indianapolis 1960.

COHEN, P. S., *Modern Social Theory*, Heineman Educational Books, London 1968.

COMTE, AUGUSTE, *System of Positive Polity*, B. Franklin, Longmans Green & Co., London 1875, Vol. 4, Book 6, Ch. 3.

COSER, L. A., *The Functions of Social Conflict*, Routledge and Kegan Paul, London 1956.

CRICK, B., "Freedom as Politics", in P. Laslett (ed.), *Philosophy, Politics and Society: A Collection*, B. Blackwell, Oxford 1963.

DAHL, R. A., *A Preface to Democratic Theory*, University of Chicago Press, Chicago 1956.

—— *Political Opposition in Western Democracies*, Yale University Press, New Haven 1966.

—— *Who Governs? Democracy and Power in an American City*, Yale University Press, New Haven 1961.

DAHL, R. A. and LINDBLOM, C. E., *Politics, Economics and Welfare: Planning and Politico-Economic Systems Resolved into Basic Social Premises*, Harper, New York 1953.

DAHRENDORF, R., *Class and Class Conflict in Industrial Society*, Routledge and Kegan Paul, London 1959.

D'ENTREVES, P. A., *The Notion of the State*, Clarendon Press, Oxford 1967.

DURKHEIM, EMILE, *Socialism and Saint Simon (le Socialisme)*; edited and with an introduction by A. W. Gouldner, Collier Books, New York; Collier-Macmillan Ltd, London 1962.

ECKSTEIN, H., *A Theory of Stable Democracy*, Center of International Studies, Princeton University (Research Monograph No. 10), Princeton, N.J. 1961.

ETZIONE, A., *The Active Society: A Theory of Societal and Political Processes*, Collier-Macmillan, London; Free Press, New York 1968.

FRANKEL, C., *The Democratic Prospect*, Harper and Row, New York 1962.

FRIEDRICH, C. J., *Man and His Government*, McGraw Hill, New York 1963.

—— *The New Belief in the Common Man*, Little, Brown, Boston 1942.

GELLNER, E., "Democracy and Industrialisation", *Archives Europeennes de Sociologie*, VIII, 1967.

GOUGH, J. W., *The Social Contract*, Clarendon Press, 2nd edn, Oxford 1967.

HAAS, E., *Beyond the Nation State: Functionalism and International Organisation*, Stanford University Press, Stanford, California 1964.

HOOKER, RICHARD, *Of the Laws of Ecclesiastical Polity*, in the *Works*, with an account of his life and death by Isaac Walton, Clarendon Press, Oxford 1865, 2 vols.

JOUVENAL, BERTRAND DE, *Sovereignty*, tr. J. F. Huntington, University Press, Chicago; University Press, Cambridge 1957.

KEY, V. O., *Public Opinion and American Democracy*, A. A. Knopf, New York 1961.

KORNHAUSER, W. A., *The Politics of Mass Society*, Routledge and Kegan Paul, London 1960; Free Press, New York 1968.

LINDBLOM, C. E., *The Intelligence of Democracy: Decision Making Through Mutual Adjustment*, Free Press, New York 1965.

LIPSET, SEYMOUR MARTIN, *Political Man*, Doubleday, Garden City, New York 1960; Heinemann, London 1960.

LOCKWOOD, R. A., "Some Comments on the Social System", *British Journal of Sociology*, Vol. 7, 1956.

McILWAIN, C. H., *The Growth of Political Thought in the West from the Greeks to the End of the Middle Ages*, Macmillan, New York 1955.

MACRIDIS, R. C. (ed.), *Modern Political Systems*, Prentice Hall, Englewood Cliffs, N.J. 1963, Vol. 1.

MARSHALL, T. H., *Citizenship and Social Class and Other Essays*, Cambridge University Press, Cambridge 1950.

MILL, J. S., *Bentham and Coleridge*, edited by F. R. Leavis, Chatto and Windus, London 1950.

MILL, J. S., *A System of Logic*, new impression, Longmans Green, New York 1900.

MILLS, C. WRIGHT, *The Power Elite*, Oxford University Press, New York 1956.

MOSCA, G., *The Ruling Class*, edited and revised with an introduction by A. Livingston, translated by H. D. Kahn, McGraw Hill, New York 1968.

MYRDAL, G., *Value in Social Theory: A Selection of Essays on Methodology*, edited by P. Streeton, Routledge and Kegan Paul, London 1958.

NEWCOMBE, T. M., "The Study of Consensus", in R. K. Merton, L. Broom and L. S. Cottrell, Jnr (eds) under the auspices of the American Sociological Society, *Sociology Today*, Basic Books, New York 1959.

PARSONS, TALCOTT, *Essays in Sociological Theory*, rev. edn., Free Press, New York 1965.

—— "The Power Elite", review article, *World Politics*, Vol. 10, October 1967.

—— *The Social System*, Free Press, Glencoe, Ill. 1959; Tavistock Publications, London 1952.

—— *The Structure of Social Action*, 2nd edn, Free Press, Glencoe, Ill. 1949.

PARTRIDGE, P. H., "Politics, Philosophy, Ideology", in A. Quinton (ed.), *Political Philosophy*, Oxford University Press, London 1967.

PLAMENATZ, J., GRIFFITH, E. S., PENNOCK, J. R., "Cultural Prerequisites to a Successfully Functioning Democracy", *American Political Science Review*, Vol. 50, March 1956.

PROTHRO, J. W. and GRIGG, C. W., "Fundamental Principles of Democracy: Bases of Agreement and Disagreement", *Journal of Politics*, Vol. 22, May 1960.

PYE, L., *Aspects of Political Development*, Little, Brown, Boston 1966.

ROUSSEAU, J. J., *The Social Contract and Discourses*; translated with an introduction by G. D. H. Cole, Dent, London 1916.

SABINE, G. H., *A History of Political Theory*, 3rd edn, rev. and enl., G. G. Harrap, London 1944.

SCHONFIELD, A., *Modern Capitalism*, Oxford University Press, London 1965.

SCHUMPETER, J., *Capitalism Socialism and Democracy*, 3rd edn, Allen and Unwin, London 1950.

SHILS, E. A., "Centre and Periphery", in *The Logic of Personal Knowledge: Essays Presented to Michael Polanyi on His 70th Birthday*, Routledge and Kegan Paul, London 1961.

—— *The Torment of Secrecy: the Background and Consequences of American Security Policies*, Free Press, Glencoe, Ill. 1956.

SOREL, G., *Reflections on Violence*, authorised translation by T. E. Hume, Allen and Unwin, London 1925.

TOCQUEVILLE, ALEXIS DE, *Democracy in America*, edited by Phillips Bradley, Alfred A. Knopf, New York 1946.

TRUMAN, D. B., *The Governmental Process*, Alfred A. Knopf, New York 1951.

TULLOCH, G. and BUCHANAN, J. M., *Calculus of Consent: Logical Foundations of Constitutional Democracy*, University of Michigan Press, Ann Arbor 1962.

TUSSMAN, J., *Obligation and the Body Politic*, Oxford University Press, New York 1960.

VAUGHAN, C. E., *Studies in the History of Political Philosophy Before and After Rousseau*, edited by A. G. Little, Manchester University Press 1925, 2 vols.

WEBER, M., *The Theory of Social and Economic Organization*, translated by A. M. Henderson and T. Parsons; edited with an introduction by T. Parsons, Free Press, Glencoe, Ill. 1947; M. Hodge, London 1947; Oxford University Press, New York 1949.

WILLHOITE, FRED W., "Political Order and Consensus", *Western Political Quarterly*, Vol. 16, 1963.

WOODHOUSE, A. S. P. (ed.), *Puritanism and Liberty: Being the Army Debates (1647–9) from the Clarke Manuscripts*, selected and edited with an introduction by A. S. P. Woodhouse, J. M. Dent, London 1951.

Index

Acquiescence: apathetic or habitual, 32-3; habitual following of established practice, form of, 56, 59; under duress, 32; states of, 41

Action: 'direct', 132; voluntary or deliberate, 36

Almond, G., 111

Althusius, 17

Aristotle, 11-12: his conception of community, 12; his conception of the *polis*, 12; *Politics*, 11

Authority: granting of permission for exercise of, 40; 'legitimacy' of, 23

Bagehot, Walter, 55, 62

Balfour, Arthur James, 1st earl of, 62, 98, 108

Behaviour: conforming, 33, 80; political and social conforming, 31-2; social and political affected by relationships, 38; traditional, 33

Bendix, R., 52n.

Bosanquet, B., 36

Carlyle, A. J., 13

Chartists, 134

Cicero, 12, 74; *De Republica*, 12

Coercion models, 123

Cohen, P. S., 77-8; definition of consensus, 77-8; *Modern Social Theory*, 11

Coleridge, Samuel Taylor, 97

Commitment, links with consensus, 77-9

Common value system, 114, 136

Comte, Auguste, 71, 74-5, 78, 81, 82; *Cours de Philosophie Positive*, 74

Conflict models, 108, 123

Conflict theorists, 81, 85, 87, 109

Consensus: as term of social philosophy, 123-4; basic, 95, 136; connection with stability, 122; constricting influence of entrenched, 132; controversiality of, 73; cruciality of for the maintenance of functioning society, 87; decisive, 40; definition of, 71, 80, 108; different forms of, 40; 'élite', 132; forms of, 89-90; functions of, 82, 130; fundamental, 69; growth and spread of, 125-6; history of ideas of, 10-11; implementation of elements in, 118; meaning of, 74; models, 77, 108, 123; moral, 84, 86; nature of, 10; notion of, 17; permissive, 40, 72, 130, 151; political role of, 120; problems regarding social characteristics, 76-7; replacing consent as concept of democratic regime structure, 72; role of, 90-1, 121; social, 69; supportive, 40, 42-3, 59, 72, 93, 130, 150; theories of, 71; theorists, 50, 75, 81, 82, 85, 109, 119, 125; value, 77, 105, 119, 139; views regarding constitutional values and issues of policy, 121; wide range of reference of, 73

Consent: ambiguity of, 9-10; by fiat, 45; coincidences with liberal parliamentary democracy, 45; complexity in defining, 17, 26-7; constitution of, 60; diffused, 65; 'distribution' of, 49; doctrine of popular, 15, 19, 151; express, 16; forms of, 44, 47, 50; 'gradations' of, 46, 50–1; history of ideas of, 10–11; idea of, 28–9, 48; intensity of, 66–7; intention of, 24; internalization as type of, 34; manifestation in society, 49; manipulation of minds, type of, 32; meaning of, 31, 37; medieval ideas of, 14; method of, 57, 59–60; permissive, 63, 72; 'reflected', 62; status of, 139, 152; stronger forms of, 63; supportive, 72; 'tacit', 21–2; views on, 44–5

Consultation and negotiation, machinery of, 65

Crick, Professor, B., 37–8, 46

Dahl, R. A., 60, 90, 103, 127–30, 132: queries appropriateness of two-party system, 127–8; *Political Opposition in Western Democracies*, 129

Dahrendorf, Ralf, 87

Deliberate choice element, 34

Democracy and democracies: affected by combination of consensus and consent, 110; consent as constituent element of, 23; development of Western, 128; 'direct', 36; doctrine of, 95; domination by few organized political parties, 117; extension of ways of living, 105; high degree of discipline demanded by some, 114; ideology of modern, 15, 48; industrial, 141; influences affecting, 100; meaning of, 59; model of, 60; 'polyarchal', 60, 62, 64, 68, 133, 147; special problem of, 97; spread of, 30–1; values of, 96–119; widespread political participation as condition of, 146

Democratic ideology, degree of, characterized by incoherence, 113

Democratic polity, 56, 127, 133; constituents of, 133–4; fundamentals as basic rules of, 99

Democratic societies, complexity of value systems of, 114

Democratic systems: citizens' attitudes, confusion of towards, 112; ignorance of by large proportion of community, 111–12; 'participation', 135, 136, 137; political indifference to, 112, 148–9; stability of, 96, 98, 106

Democratic values: levels of, 110–11; no universal agreement as to, 113

Democrats, distinction between types of, 112

De Tocqueville, Alexis, 71

Diffusion, process of, 105–6

Discretion, or 'act of secrecy', 145

Discussion, restrictions on power of, 144

Dissensus, 82, 87, 118, 120: importance of ideological, 134; moral, 84; role of, 121

Dissent, absence of, 67; effective opportunities for, 67; free elections as means of reducing, 143–4; open, 68; right to, 69

'Divine right' development of doctrine of, 14–15

Durkheim, Emile, 71, 81, 84

Eckstein, Professor H., 92, 94; views on stability, 92, 94

Economic growth, 107

Elections, 41: free, 143–4, 146; traditional or habitual voting, 41–2

Electoral process as institutional centre of government by consent, 40

Elites, 41, 54, 72, 93, 116–18, 121: appreciation of basic values of democracy, 116; important role of, 58

Empiricism, 135

Franchise, widening of, 28

Friedrich, Professor C. J., 54, 92, 98, 108, 124: rejects agreement about fundamentals, 92, 108; theory regarding supporting of constitutional order by popular consensus, 54, 124

Fundamentals, agreement about, 62, 92, 95, 96, 98, 108, 140

General Strike of 1926, 104
Gewirth, Professor A., 56–7, 59; exposition of theory of consent, 56–7
Gough, J. W., 12–13
Government: duties to identify problems and issues, 150; duty of, 141; increasing extent of interaction with individuals and groups, 93; must make judgement between consent and dissent, 152; notions of functions of, 41; policy of non-interference, 101; popular participation in, 27; representative, 135; respect for powerful minorities, 102; should employ authority to make own decisions, 142; should use initiative, 150
'Government by consent of governed', 9, 18, 19, 25, 26, 28–31, 34–42, 50–1, 56, 58–60, 64, 67, 135, 136, 140–52
Green, A. S., 36
Grotius, 17
Groups, dissident, 57

Haas, E., 92
Hitler, Adolf, 44
Hobbes, Thomas, 19
Hooker, Richard, 15–18, 21, 72, 74: his traditions of thought, 15–16, 21; *The Laws of Ecclesiastical Polity*, 15
Horowitz, I. L., 75
Human society, dependence on voluntary agreement, 10
Hume, David, 20

Ideologies, 135
Immunities, 61
Incrementalism, 127, 138
Individualism, 12, 19
Individuals, right of, 12
'Initiative', 39
Instability, 123

Institutions, shaping of by pressures, 113–14
Internalization, 34–5, 79; of values and norms, 78

Jehovah's Witnesses, banning of, 102
Jouvenel, Robert de, 117
Justinian, 14

Key, Professor V. O., 40, 42, 59, 72, 74, 77, 93–4, 130, 150; *Public Opinion and American Democracy*, 40
Kingship, medieval ideas and doctrine of, 13, 21

Laski, Professor H. J., 62, 99–100
Lenin, Vladimir Ilyich, 99
Leninists, 125, 129
Lipset, S. M., 52n.
Locke, John, 17, 18–23, 27–31, 33, 61, 72: advocates supplementary ideas, 20–1; his concept of consent, 30; his 'tacit' consent, 21–3, 33, 72; theory, 19–20; view that functions of government were minimal, 24–5

Majority rule, 135
Mandate, constitution of, 139–40
Marshall, T. H., 105; *Citizenship and Social Class*, 105
Marsiglio of Padua, 14; *Defensor Pacis*, 14
Marx, Karl, 81, 99, 107, 108; his analysis of capitalism, 107
Marxists, 85, 86, 124, 129
McClosky, H. J., 96, 118–19; views on consensus, 118–19
McIlwain, I. C. H., 12; expounding of Aristotle's conception of the *polis*, 12
Membership, 'involuntary', 30
Menzies, Sir Robert, 62
Merton, R. K., 55
Mill, John Stuart, 75, 97–8, 104, 134–5: conditions of permanent political society, 97–8; definition

of consensus, 75; *Liberty*, 134; *System of Logic*, 75

Mills, C. Wright, 83

Minorities, 106

Myrdal, G., 85; *An American Dilemma*, 85

Nicholas of Cusa, 14, 30

Non-interference, 101–2

Parsons, Talcott, 78, 83–5, 91; *The Structure of Social Action*, 83–4

Plamenatz, Professor J., 37, 41, 42; *Consent, Freedom and Political Obligation*, 37, 41

Plato, 11, 12; conception of community, 12

Pluralism, 148–9

Pluralists, 147

Political apathy, 133, 148

Political authority: basic acceptance of basic structure of, 54; claims in share of exercise of by wide communities, 28; constituents of, 38; dependence on relationships, 45; the granted permission of, 35–6; the notion of creation of, 10, 13–15

Political parties, images of, 63

Political societies: description of, 94; stability of, 91

Politics: consensus, 67, 73, 115; non-ideological style, 128; social fluidity in, 29

Popular election, doctrine of, 13

Power, 52–3

Power and authority, 26–7, 82–3

Pressure group, 147

Pufendorf, 17

Putney Debates, 18, 105

Rainborough, Colonel George, 18, 105, 134

'Referendum', 39

Renan, Ernest, 22

Roman law tradition, 13–14

Roosevelt, President Franklin D., 53, 62

Rousseau, Jean-Jacques, 24, 36

Schumpeter, Joseph, 62, 100

Shils, E., 63, 87, 89, 93, 114–15, 126–7

'Silent allowance', 16, 72, 74

Social contract doctrine, 11, 15, 17, 19, 20: distinction between 'nature' and 'convention', 11; objections to, 20

Social contract theorists, 10–11, 17–18, 28–9

Social development, importance of, 106

Social norms, 83

Social organization: conflict models of, 88; differing areas or levels of, 51–70

Socialization, 33–4, 43, 54

Societies: degrees of passivity and activity in, 43–4; functioning, 87; generalizations concerning, 122; important differences of degree between, 39; prevailing forms of consent in, 46–7

Society: characteristics of, 76; civil, 63; extent governed by democratic values, 131; maintenance of by widespread community support, 101; participative, 63; wide diversity of religious creeds in, 99

Socrates, 11

Sorel, Georges, 137

Stabilities: basic, 50; connection with consensus, 122; importance of role played by consensus in, 89, 123; level of, 88–9; non-consensual conditions of, 119

States: authoritarian and totalitarian, 43; characteristics of, 38; function of, 126; industrial dependence on majority consent, 46

Strategies, coalescent, 130–2

Structural opposition, decline of, 133

Tolerance, as mark of democracy, 115

Trade Disputes Act, 1927, 104

Trade Unions: ability to exert power, 103; as part of industrial democratic society, 104; attempts at making illegality of, 102–3

United States: ambiguities in attachment to 'American creed', 85; disaffection of ethnic and cultural minorities, 111; dissent in, 69; opposition to constitutional rules in, 53; promotion of cult of 'the constitution', 56

Verba, S., 111

Weber, M., 33, 55; his 'traditional authority', 33, 55
Weimar regime, 68
Welfare state, concept of, 126
Wildman, John, 18–19, 38, 134